INFINITE PATTERN

GINGKO PRESS

INFINITE PATTERN

ISBN 978-1-58423-495-1

First Published in the United States of America by Gingko Press
by arrangement with Sandu Publishing Co., Limited

Gingko Press, Inc.
1321 Fifth Street
Berkeley, CA 94710 USA
Tel: (510) 898 1195
Fax: (510) 898 1196
Email: books@gingkopress.com
www.gingkopress.com

Copyright © 2012 by SANDU PUBLISHING

Sponsored by Design 360°
– Concept and Design Magazine

Edited and produced by
Sandu Publishing Co., Ltd.

Book design, concepts & art direction by
Sandu Publishing Co., Ltd.

sandu.publishing@gmail.com
www.sandupublishing.com

Cover pattern by Romualdo Faura

Printed and bound in China

PREFACE

Chez Valois

Chez Valois, a Montreal-based agency, designs premium brands with a real commercial edge. Since 2005, the award-winning team has been offering its expertise in brand strategy, brand identity, and visual/structural packaging design. Chez Valois ensures the cohesion and success of the brands they work with. They believe that our image-conscious nation has always paid more attention to surfaces than cores. However, our society is always in search of authenticity. This is why the team believes that businesses need constructive imaginations in order to deeply connect with people and produce sustainable changes. Their design process is simple, yet profound: sense, imagine, and construct.

What is the common thread between the stripes of a zebra, the pistils of a dandelion, the rocks of the Giant's Causeway, the scales of an emerald tree boa, and even the iris of your eyes? Think carefully! Alternating black and white curved lines, small, fluffy white stars, hexagonal rock columns along a coast, a hyper-orderly grid of green and white diamonds, or colour filaments arranged around a small black circle... they all have something in common. They are naturally-occurring patterns. These harmonious structures are proof that patterns are not exclusively the work of humans. In fact, they have always existed in millions of forms. From the sand dunes drawn by the Dzhari winds, to the veins on a leaf, to the honeycombs of the beehive, patterns surround us. Designers are not ignorant of this, and consciously or unconsciously, they breathe them in and derive inspiration from them to create repetitions of shapes.

Human beings have always been fascinated by patterns. As early as the thirteenth century, mathematicians were captivated by them and tried to explain the phenomena in a rational and scientific way. One of them, an Italian mathematician by the name of Fibonacci, became obsessed with these repetitive, aesthetic phenomena found in the likes of the fractals of Romanesco broccoli, the petals of artichokes, the needles on cacti, the faces of sunflowers, and the scales of pine cones. Fibonacci proposed a mathematical theory to account for these natural patterns. If you take a closer look at a sunflower, you will see that the seeds form sets of spirals that can go in both directions. Fibonacci discovered that these aesthetic phenomena were organized in a pattern of numbers (0, 1, 1, 2, 3, 5, 8, 13, 21, 34, 55, 89, 144...) today known as the Fibonacci sequence. Basically, each number in the series is the result of adding the previous two together, and as the numbers increase, the ratio between them gets closer and closer to 1.6180339887, the Golden Ratio used in many fields of the arts! Fantastic!

Patterns are naturally present at all scales, from micro to macro, whether it is in the organization of our DNA, the cells that form our bodies, or the families, groups, and neighborhoods that together form our cities. All of these are complex organizations that, most often, are composed of only one or a few simple repetitive shapes.

To the joy of all of us who hold this book in our hands, patterns are not the exclusive realm of mathematicians and scientists. It is not a sterile science. Rather, it is a playground found at the intersection of creativity and rigour. Repetition, enumeration, juxtaposition, superimposition, processing, modulation, offsetting, rotation, formation, amplitude, colour... there are a myriad of ways to build rhythm, texture, and richness from patterns. The mere idea of them is a trigger for creativity. Patterns are simply fascinating. We, as human beings, express our undying love for them in the way we create, recreate, seek, interpret, and rethink them. And so it is not surprising that they can be found everywhere, from paintings, sculptures, crafts, graphic designs, interior designs, industrial designs, architecture, and music all the way to fashion. Each is unique in style, stemming from diverse cultures, eras, or influencing trends.

Go ahead! Produce a shape, then duplicate it, play with it, rotate it, flip it, colour it. One shape becomes 100, then 400, then 7688, evolving into an entirely new structure, a landscape. Now start again. Designers and the creative process can form an infinite number of patterns, thanks to computers, which operate on the basis of repetitions of 1s and 0s! If we look more closely, even the pixels create an organized pattern! If we then go wild, and take a magnifying glass to the beautiful examples featured in this book, we realize that all printed images are composed of four superimposed structured dot grids of each process colour! Let me tell you, we can lose our minds in this!

Long live patterns! Turning to the specific subject of this book, their graphic applications alone are endless. They are found on everything from food packaging, to business cards, to wrapping paper, embedded in the sheets of fine papers, or better still, knitted into a warm sweater by your grandmother! Patterns offer a subtle way to bring moods, textures, flavours, or personalities to any item. Furthermore, their enveloping nature brings a treasured feeling to everything they cover.

Take for example the famous "LV" monogram, the pattern of which was invented in 1896 by French luggage maker Georges Vuitton, son of Louis. It has become an iconic brand symbol, transcending over a century of fashion. Moreover, the quatrefoils and flowers associated with the interlaced "L" and "V" graphics convey the essence of the brand. Another interesting fact: the Celts used the tartan (criss-crossing of horizontal and vertical line patterns of multiple colours) to identify the origin of one's family or clan. The pattern that lends itself to a brand, idea, or message can become an alluring factor, capturing the enthusiasm of the ones who indulge in looking at it.

I could not pinpoint the source of inspiration or the starting point of each of the creations presented in this book. However, I do know what unites them all: the absolute pleasure we, the designers, had in multiplying shapes we created from our own imaginations.

In my opinion, almost any shape has a potential destiny in a pattern, and I love that! Taking a trip on the wild side, I begin to imagine small geometric or organic motifs, spreads of colour, beautiful curved lines, and psychedelic moirés suddenly emerging from my screen and coming alive, dancing under the rhythm of an electro-pop number. Better yet, I dream of a spray that could paint my fondest patterns on any surface! I can see myself in a plane, spraying an organic leaf motif of various shades of green over a deforested landscape from the sky!

Utopian dreams of a world completely painted in my own colours aside, I must confess that it is rather pleasing to see my patterns brought together with my colleagues' best works in this great book. The beautiful selection of works here are as diverse in nature as they are in their applications and countries of origin. I am convinced that the reader will find inspiration in this book, not to mention happiness.

Happy pattern blasting!

Michel Vrois

CONTENTS

GFSmith

DESIGN: SEA DESIGN

SEA did the art direction, design, and generative coding for a digital paper promotion for GFSmith.

Generative processes combined code with pre-determined colour palettes to create a series of 10,000 unique digital prints.

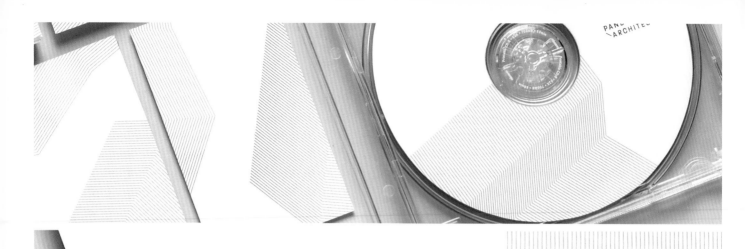

Pandolfini Architects

AGENCY: MAYTHORPE
CREATIVE DIRECTION: SPENCER BITCON
ART DIRECTION: JOSHUA LOUGHLAND

Focused on producing conceptual, sculptural solutions for a range of residential, commercial, and urban design projects, Pandolfini Architects engaged Maythorpe to develop a design concept that would reflect the company's style and approach. An intricate set of patterns were created to echo Pandolfini's use of line in creating form and space. Maythorpe also incorporated colour gradients to represent the play of light on architectural structures. The patterns were then applied to printed products and the company's website, often encroaching space traditionally left void to further reflect the firms unique approach.

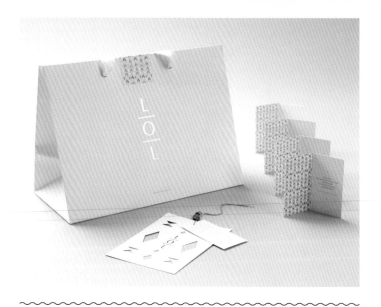

LOL

DESIGN: FACETOFACEDESIGN

Facetofacedesign created the brand identity for LOL, a multi brand boutique in Brussels.

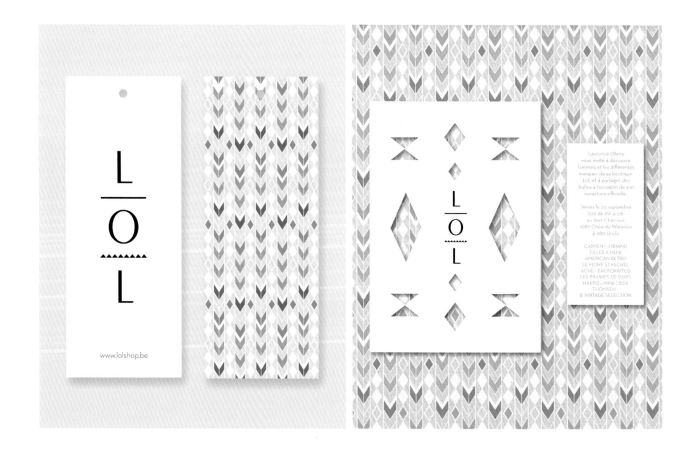

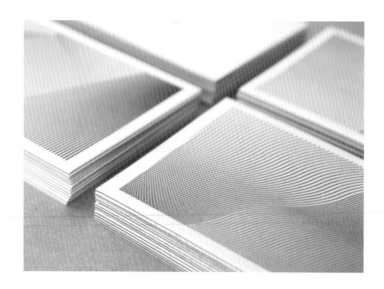

Rítmia. Music Therapy

DESIGN: ATIPUS

Atipus designed a series of patterns for social music therapist and educator Celia Castillo. The patterns are based on the rhythmic exercises Celia develops. The basic aim is to provoke different moods in her patients.

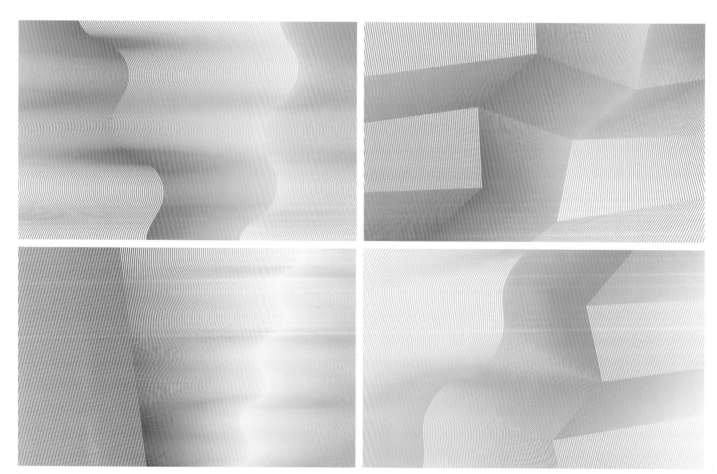

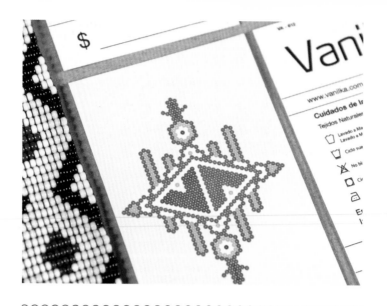

~~~~~~

Vanilka

~~~~~~

AGENCY: SINGULAR

Fashion is one of the most unique ways in which individuals can express their creativity. Vanilka (an up and coming clothing line from Mexico) expresses itself through a geometrical tour.

Singular was approached to develop the brand for the young atelier but their involvement expanded way beyond that; they became involved with the advert campaigns, photo-shoots, print ads, stationery applications, and art direction.

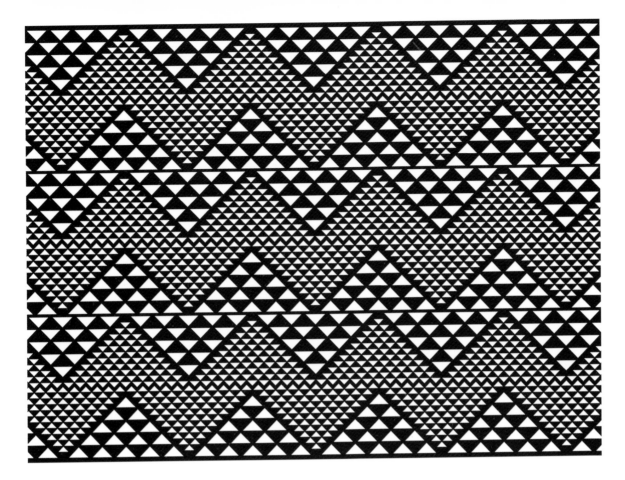

Montenegro Fast-food Restaurant

DESIGN: KATERYNA MISHYNA
ILLUSTRATION: KATERYNA MISHYNA

Kateryna Mishyna developed this project while completing her master's degree in communication design. The assignment was to create a new graphic image for any restaurant by redesigning an image forming element. Kateryna picked a Montenegro fast-food restaurant because she saw a great deal of unfulfilled potential in it. Her investigation was mainly centred on Montenegro national handicraft, especially on their rich textile design. Therefore Kateryna selected some of their motifs and reproduced them repeatedly, creating combinations of patterns. The original drawings were made with nib pen and watercolors. The prevalent color is red, echoing the Montenegro national costumes.

MONTENEGRO
GURMAN GYORSÉTTEREM

Neige Packaging

DESIGN: MICHEL VALOIS
AGENCY: CHEZ VALOIS

Inspired by the technique used to make ice wine and Québec's climate, Neige (which means "snow" in English) ice cider was born out of the province's terroir, which has the extreme winter temperatures needed to produce the necessary concentration of sugar. The cidery La Face Cachée de la Pomme approached Chez Valois to redesign the brand's image and packaging for the product line.

The goal was to reaffirm the position of this premium brand as a leader and trendsetter in the ice cider category in addition to boosting its recognition on the international market. To achieve this, a clean and minimalist design was based on a pattern of snowflakes that can be found throughout the product line. A lot of subtle elements were also included in the design of the packaging, such as a peel-off label on the back of the bottle that allows the inclusion of more information on the history of the cidery and the ice cider fabrication process. Custom packing tape was also created to indicate the contents of the shipping boxes.

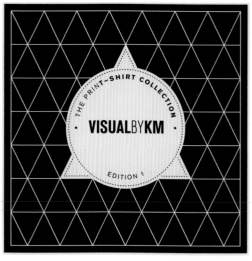

Visual by KM

DESIGN: KILÓMETRO ESTUDIO

Visual by KM is a limited edition line of T-shirts, developed by Kilómetro Estudio for its clothes' brand KM.

The collection's identity system was developed from a pattern built by the repetition of triangles.

Each pack makes up a subsystem that is part of the main system. The form of the pattern represents a morphologic synthesis of the essential structure of each T-shirt's design.

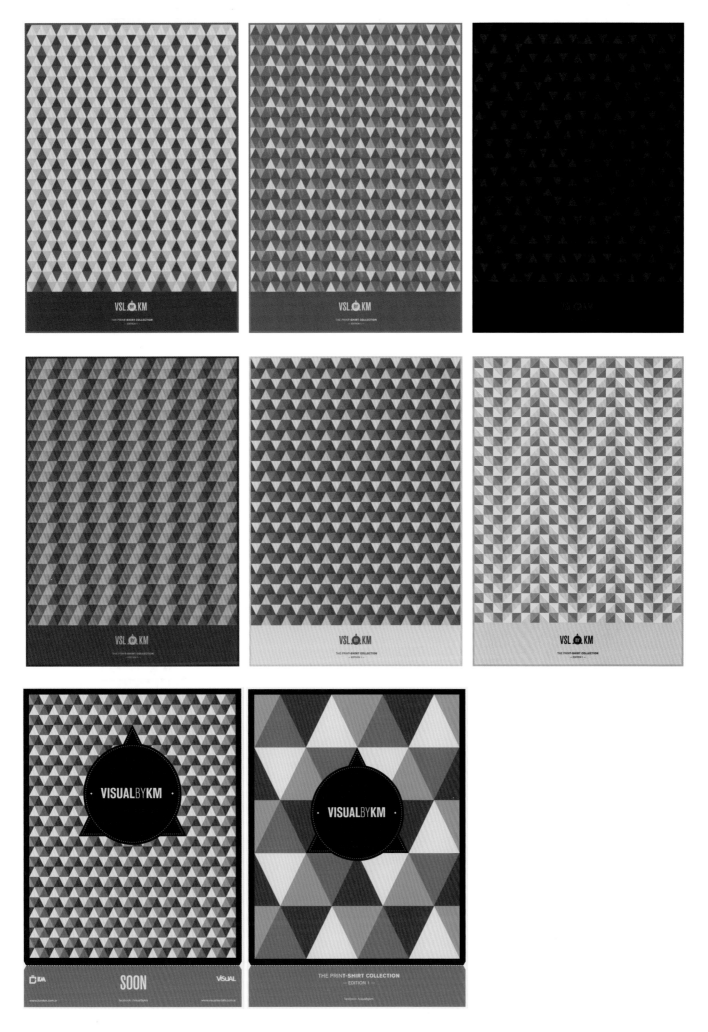

Tricolette

DESIGN: KENTLYONS

KentLyons developed Tricolette's brand, signage, packaging, stationery, business cards and flyers, store signage, and website. The retail store is located in London, NW8.

KentLyons was asked to avoid tired associations with knitting; a more modern approach was needed in order to appeal to new and young knitters as well as experienced ones.

Tricolette's brand logo is made from a bespoke logotype created using 3 parallel lines. This is both a response to the name Tricolette and a reflection of the intricacy of wool and yarn. A fresh colour palette was created using three colours; pistachio, amethyst, and fushia. Copper foil adds a flourish to the stationery and the shop's storefront.

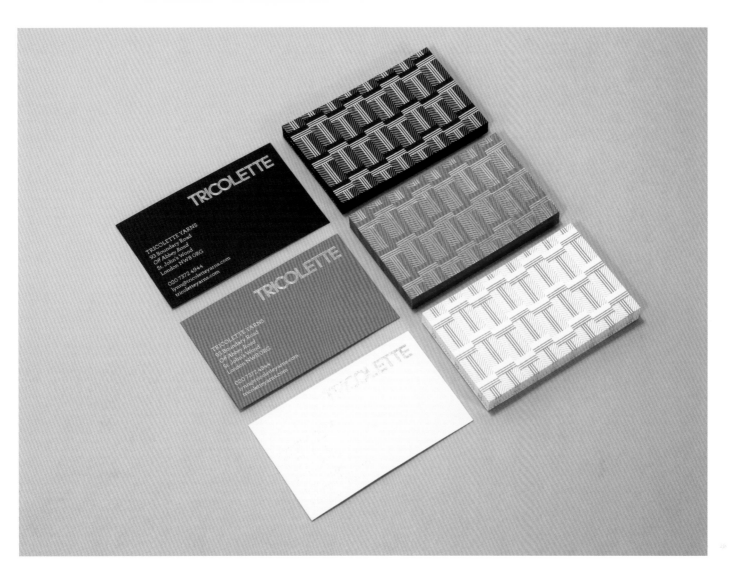

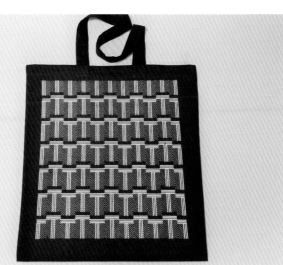

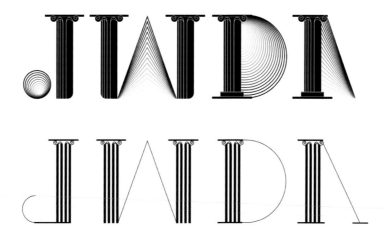

~~~~~~

James Wang

~~~~~~

AGENCY: LAVA BEIJING
ART DIRECTION: GRANT-RU LI
PHOTOGRAPHY: JIAN TAO

Lava Beijing developed the visual identity design for James Wang Design Associates, one of the best European style interior design companies in China.

They wanted to show their classical style as well as their contemporary features, so the typography design combines the most classical element of Europe—Athenian columns—with contemporary lines with a spatial feeling. Together, the lines and columns create a new beauty reminiscent of the interaction between the Louvre Pyramid and the original building.

JAMES WANG
DESIGN
ASSOCIATES
北京杰地亚建筑咨询有限公司

JAMES WANG DESIGN ASSOCIATES

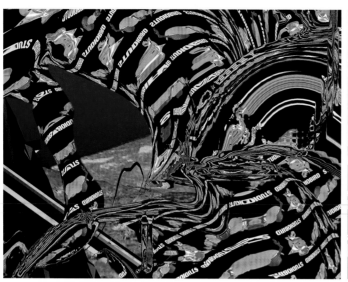

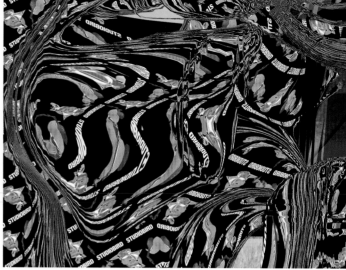

Studio Bird

DESIGN: 3 DEEP DESIGN

Matthew Bird is the founder and director of Studio Bird, a design practice delivering innovative projects that combine interior and architectural solutions. As a young practice within the Australian architectural landscape, Studio Bird is incredibly unique. It is because of the process of research, with a focus on resourcefulness and rigor, that the practice's projects are exceptional manifestations of the clients' identities that take location, budget, and social and environmental concerns into account. 3 Deep Design was engaged by Studio Bird to establish a visual identity and creative positioning that captured the essence and personality of the practice.

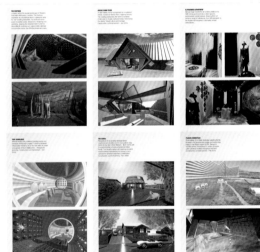

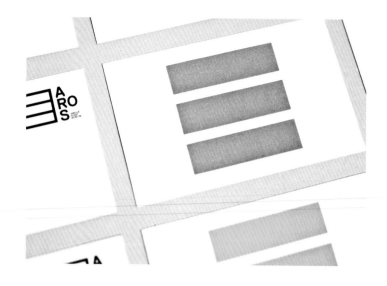

Visual identity proposal for ARoS

AGENCY: WE ARE ALL IN THIS TOGETHER™
DESIGN: DENNIS MÜLLER
PHOTOGRAPHY: ANDERS RIMHOFF
PHOTOS USED IN THE DESIGNS ARE COURTESY OF AROS
DAVID LYNCH PORTRAIT BY NADAV KANDER

ARoS (Aarhus Museum of Modern Art) is one of northern Europe's largest art museums. The designer's suggestion for a new identity was based on both the concept of the building and on ARoS's values. The architects were inspired by the "Divine Comedy," which describes Dante's travels through Hell, Purgatory, and Heaven–like the tale, the museum also consists of three levels. Hence, the logo represents the physical space.

ARoS's vision is to focus on the experience of the visitor which takes place in the physical space of the museum. Thus, the negative space in the logo is used as an additional element to symbolize the experience of the visitor.

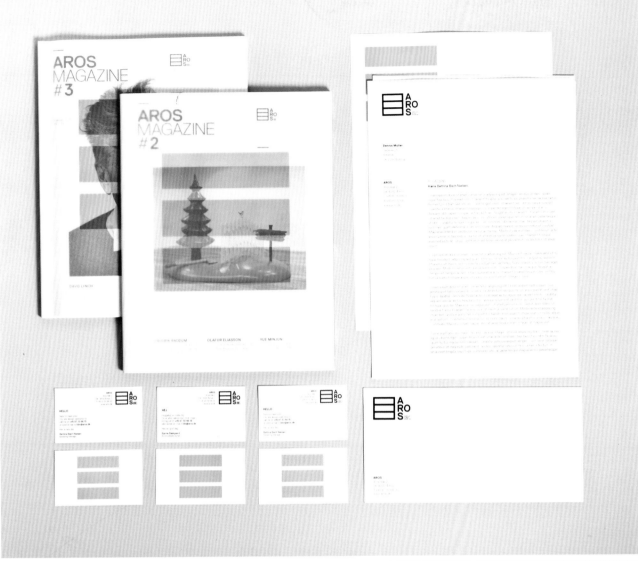

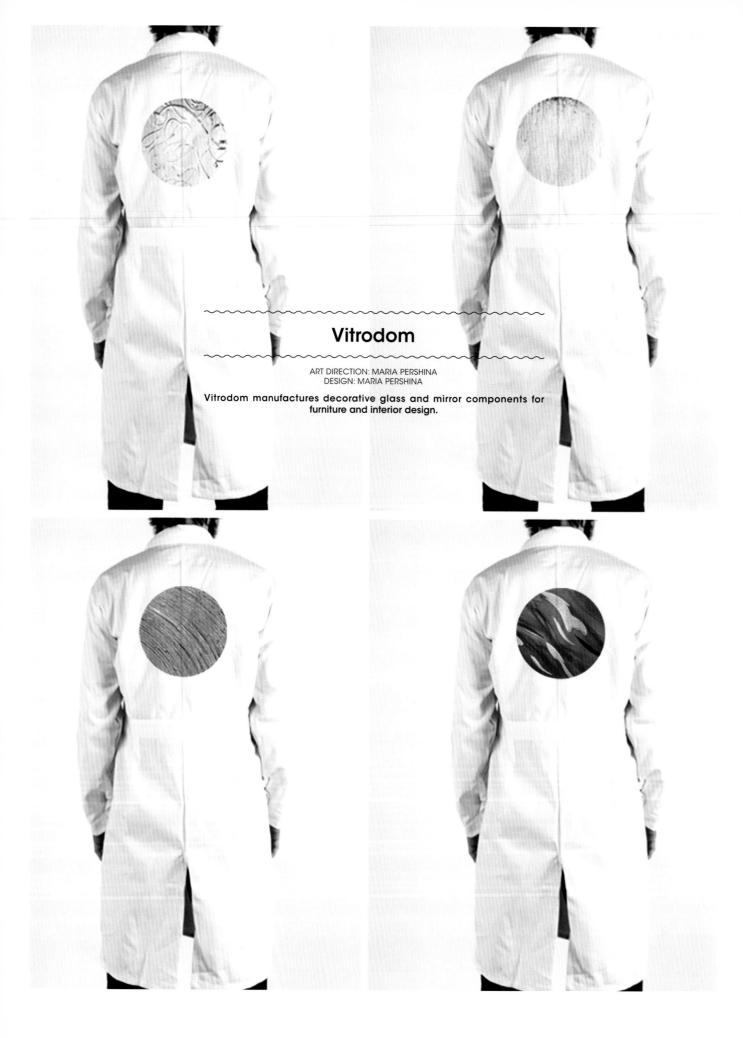

Vitrodom

ART DIRECTION: MARIA PERSHINA
DESIGN: MARIA PERSHINA

Vitrodom manufactures decorative glass and mirror components for
furniture and interior design.

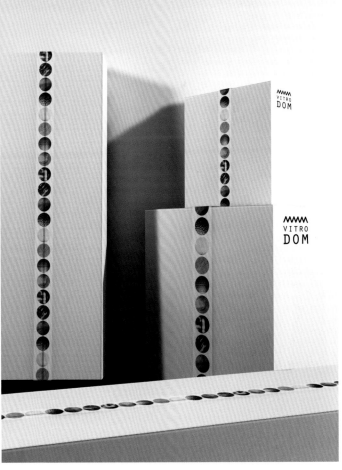

AFTER ARCO

AGENCY: LA LONJA GRÁFICA

The art fair Arco Madrid 2012 decided to expand its cultural offerings, and to this end organized a concert series lasting 2 days. The experimental groups created a collection with an exciting and eclectic character.

So La Lonja Gráfi ca decided to make a graphic image composed of two elements: typography and pattern. The pattern was developed from the font used in the logo, designed to play with the "A's" that make up the logo. The result represents the festival in a clean way that will serve for future editions.

Additionally, watercolor was included as part of the graphic image.

SEXTETO CARDÓN

AGENCY: PLACE
CREATIVE DIRECTION: ELOY KRIOKA

Sextet Cardon, a folk musical crew with six members, asked Place to help create their brand. The result symbolizes the music and adds a touch of simplicity.

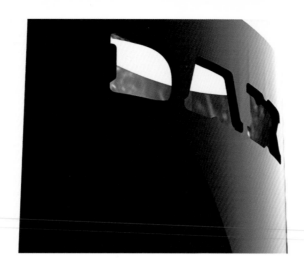

~~~~~~

DAK

~~~~~~

DESIGN: MARTIN ALBRECHT

DAK (The National Aquarium of Denmark) has the greatest species diversity of any aquarium in all of Denmark. The new identity was designed with the intimate view of this diversity the aquarium gives its visitors in mind.

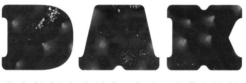

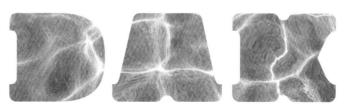

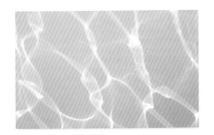

Jesper Horsted
Administrerende Direktør

jesperhorsted@DAK.dk
www.DAK.dk

DAK - Danmarks Akvarium
2 Kastrup Havn
2770 Kastrup

Telefon   (+45) 3962 3282
Fax   (+45) 3962 6416

Jesper Horsted
Administrerende Direktør

jesperhorsted@DAK.dk
www.DAK.dk

DAK - Danmarks Akvarium
2 Kastrup Havn
2770 Kastrup

Telefon   (+45) 3962 3282
Fax   (+45) 3962 6416

Jesper Horsted
Administrerende Direktør

jesperhorsted@DAK.dk
www.DAK.dk

DAK - Danmarks Akvarium
2 Kastrup Havn
2770 Kastrup

Telefon   (+45) 3962 3282
Fax   (+45) 3962 6416

Resolve

AGENCY: NEUE DESIGN STUDIO

Resolve is a supplier of cleaning and damage restoration services that has a strong commitment to its employees and their craft. Through this identity, Neue aimed to emphasize Resolve's distinct personal and proud approach in an industry that often portrays itself as sterile and devoid of emotion. The new identity is soft, warm, and professional.

Espen Tjelflaat
Salgssjef

T: 468 30 363
E: espen.tjelflaat@resolve.no

Resolve AS
Moland Vest
4994 Akland

www.resolve.no

Anne Hudalen
Daglig leder

T: 970 44 670
E: anne.hudalen@resolve.no

Resolve AS
Moland Vest
4994 Akland

www.resolve.no

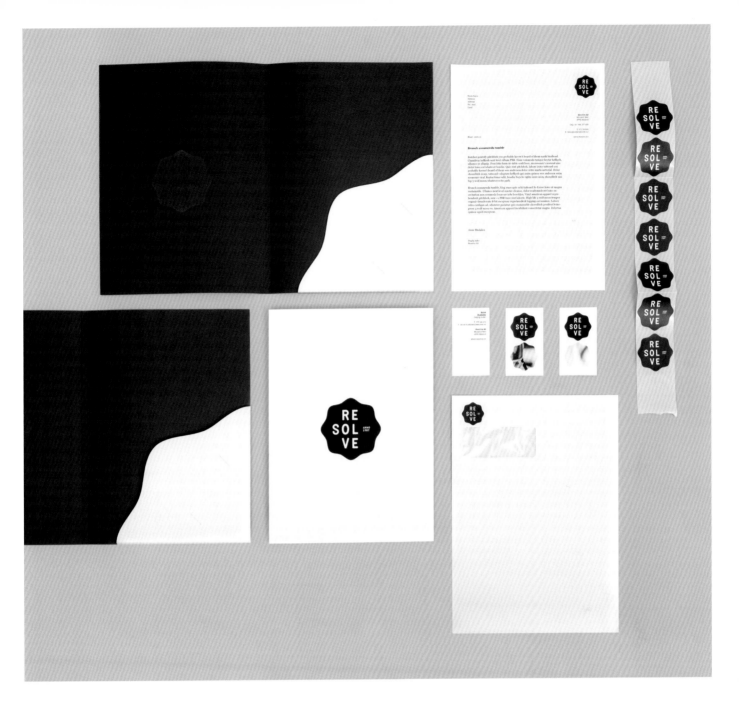

~~~~~~

OCAD University

~~~~~~

DESIGN: BRUCE MAU DESIGN

For this new identity, the Bruce Mau Design team worked collaboratively with OCAD University's Marketing & Communications team in an intensive research and engagement phase. The synthesis of this material led them to a robust set of design principles that would guide the design work. The visual identity needed to be a true reflection of what they heard and saw: an inclusive, vibrant, and vital institution built on creativity, risk, and innovation.

With this in mind, BMD asked themselves, 'can the visual identity reveal the extraordinary creative energy that lives at OCAD U?' Inspired by the iconic and transformational building designed by Alsop, BMD created a base of black and white pixel 'windows' – which form frames that hold student art and design work. It is through these `windows' that the conceptually strong, diverse, and compelling core of OCAD U may be seen. This is a dynamic and modular identity; every year, medal-winning graduating students will be invited to design a logo within the basic window framework, providing a set of logos for that year. As OCAD U grows and matures framework, a living library of identities will necessarily emerge, recording the ideas and aesthetics that have shaped our culture over time.

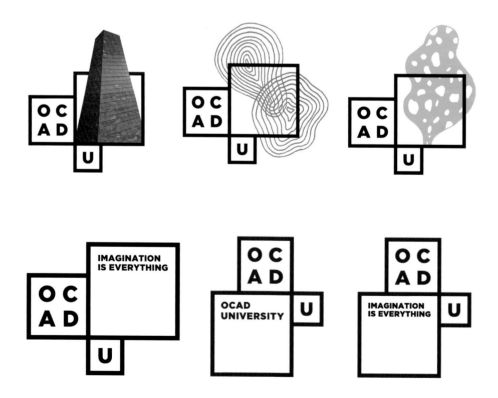

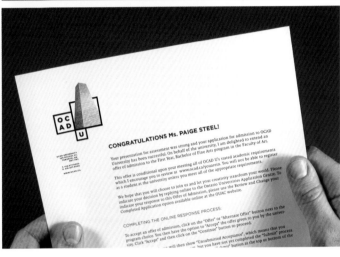

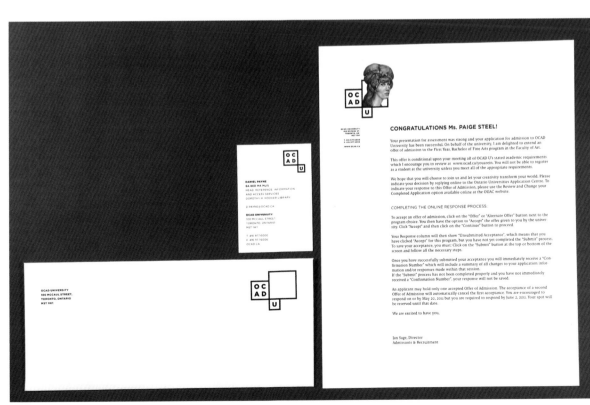

The Cupper

DESIGN: SAMANTHA KIM

Package design and branding for a coffee store concept called The Cupper. The brand is centered around the idea of individual cups of coffee and allowing customers to try variations of individually packed coffees while learning how to distinguish between flavors, bodies, and aromas. The packaging, which incorporates a unique system of shapes and colors, was created to make learning about the characteristics of coffee easy and exciting.

Fluid Project

DESIGN: DAISY DAYOUNG LEE

Daisy Dayoung Lee's thesis addresses the growing need for brands and visual identities to constantly adapt and react to dynamically changing consumer behaviors. Although consistency is one of the key qualities that branding should follow, old-fashioned, rigid identity guidelines do not meet today's diverse individuals' needs and wants anymore. Lately, the concept of the traditional client has been broadened out and far more multifarious identity designs have been requested. In this thesis, she is exploring how `flexible vocabularies in visual identity' can be conceptualized and embodied in a way that takes dynamic consumers into account and makes use of different kinds of media in order to keep it youthful. By interviewing design experts and branding professionals, she gathered and analyzed the reactions about flexible identities' benefits and challenges, and as a result, she experimented with the possibilities of flexible vocabularies in visual identity as a single test-bed project.

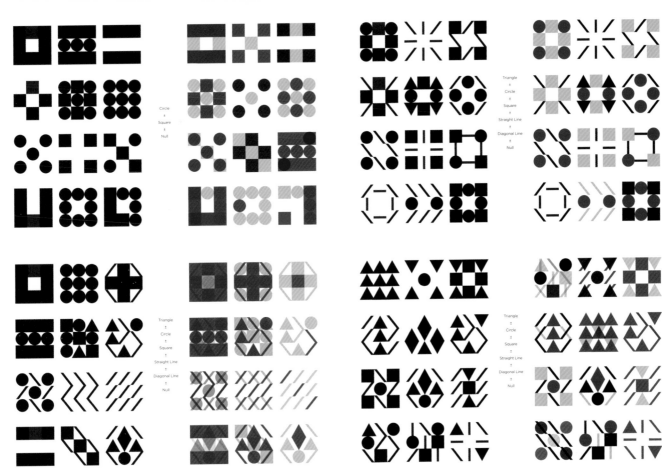

Circle
↕
Square
↕
Null

Triangle
↕
Circle
↕
Square
↕
Straight Line
↕
Diagonal Line
↕
Null

Triangle
↕
Circle
↕
Square
↕
Straight Line
↕
Diagonal Line
↕
Null

Triangle
↕
Circle
↕
Square
↕
Straight Line
↕
Diagonal Line
↕
Null

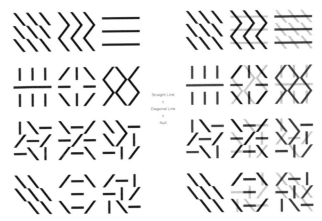

Straight Line
↕
Diagonal Line
↕
Null

the fluid conference

the fluid conference

the fluid conference

the fluid conference

the fluid conference

the fluid conference

the fluid conference

the fluid conference

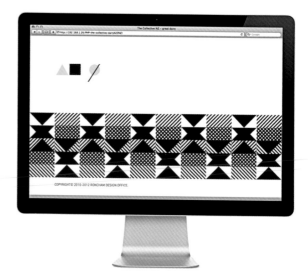

Roncham Design

DESIGN: KELVIN QU

Roncham Design, founded in 2010, is a brand consultancy based in Paris and Changzhou. The name comes from Le Corbusier's Chapelle Notre-Dame-du-Haut de Ronchamp. Roncham creates consumer experiences and advances brand value for clients. Oblique lines are added to triangles, squares, and circles, symbolizing a march from greatness to excellence.

Moscow Design Museum

AGENCY: LAVA
DESIGN: JOHAN NIJHOFF

The Moscow Design Museum is unique in several aspects. Firstly, it is the first design museum in Russia. Secondly, instead of a conventional fixed museum, the Moscow Design Museum is the world's first museum on a bus.

The identity is based on the patterns of Russian crystal, which has a unique place in Russian design history. The geometric figures form the basis fora dynamic identity which will be applied on the exhibition design, the communication, the bus, catalogues, etc.

As the museum's founding partner, Lava will also take part in various activities and exhibitions in the near future.

 МОСКОВСКИЙ МУЗЕЙ ДИЗАЙНА MOSCOW DESIGN MUSEUM

 МОСКОВСКИЙ МУЗЕЙ ДИЗАЙНА MOSCOW DESIGN MUSEUM

 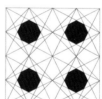 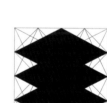

 МОСКОВСКИЙ МУЗЕЙ ДИЗАЙНА MOSCOW DESIGN MUSEUM

 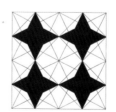 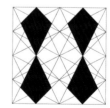

 МОСКОВСКИЙ МУЗЕЙ ДИЗАЙНА MOSCOW DESIGN MUSEUM

 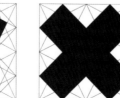 

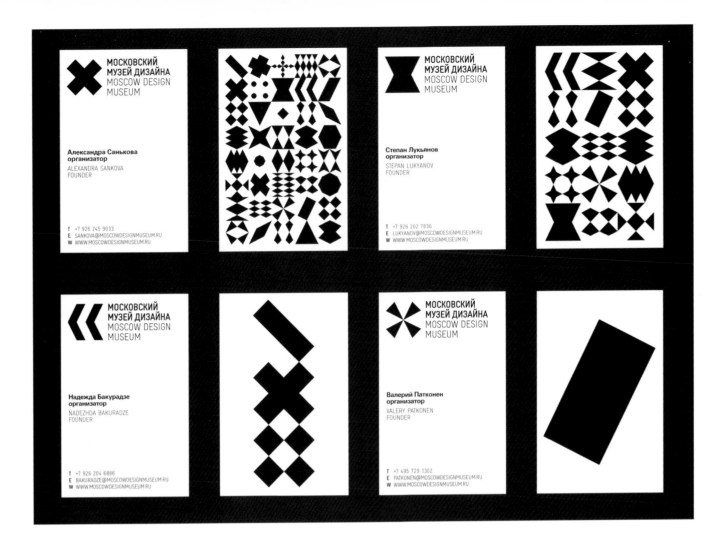

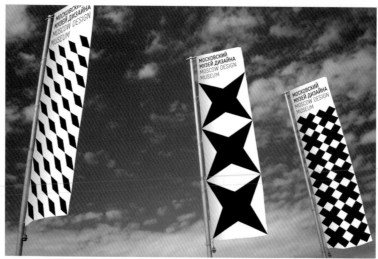

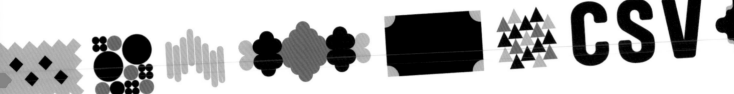

Sinfonia Varsovia Centre

AGENCY: EDGAR BĄK & ROBERT MENDEL
CREATIVE DIRECTION: EDGAR BĄK & ROBERT MENDEL

The visual identity of the cultural centre in Warsaw, Poland is forever morphing. The only fixed aspect is the guiding set of rules that governs the logo and allows it to be redesigned. The border between the logotype and the rest of the materials and stationary is blurred.

A.4 Płyta CD
A.5 Opakowanie na CD

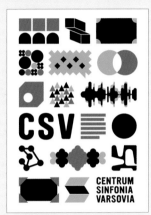

AGNIESZKA
JACOBSON–CIELECKA
T: +48 782 205 394
nazwisko@svc.pl

A.6 Wizytówka - rewers   A.6 Wizytówka - awers

~~~~~~~~~~~~~~~~~~~~~~~~~~~~~~~~~~~~~~~

Megabox

~~~~~~~~~~~~~~~~~~~~~~~~~~~~~~~~~~~~~~~

AGENCY: STUDIO FNT
CREATIVE DIRECTION: JAEMIN LEE, HEESUN KIM
DESIGN: JAEMIN LEE, HEESUN KIM, WOOGYUNG GEEL AND HOSEUNG LEE

Studio fnt developed the identity design for Megabox, one of the biggest movie theater chains in Korea. The identity design includes a symbol, a logotype, and applications from signage and tickets to beverage containers. A flexible identity system was created to represent the movie theater as an open space for entertainment and communication.

Apartment 138

AGENCY: HYPERAK
DESIGN: DEROY PERAZA
PHOTOGRAPHY: NOAH KALINA

Hyperak worked closely with Apartment 138 owner Ted Mann to convert his vision for this one-time apartment turned hip Carroll Gardens restaurant into a fully realized brand. They stayed true to the space's history, using the building's original address plaque and vintage wallpaper as visual springboards for the logo, custom place mats, engraved wood coasters, and elegant signage.

Upii Cupcakes

DESIGN: REJANE DAL BELLO

Upii cupcakes has established a great reputation among party lovers and sweets consumers. Celebration has always been the core of the company's vision, which is conveyed through its marketing materials, signage, and packaging. Upii is a cupcake company that caters to a wide range of clients from children's parties to weddings.

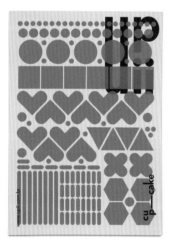

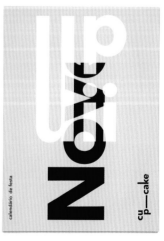

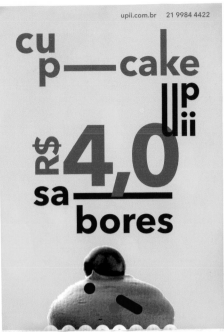

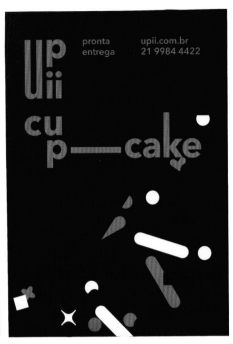

Polluted Records

AGENCY: BRANCH
DESIGN: TIJL SCHNEIDER

Polluted Records wanted an identity that was strong, bold, and contemporary.

By using pause and stop symbols, Branch created a marque that reflected the industrial name.

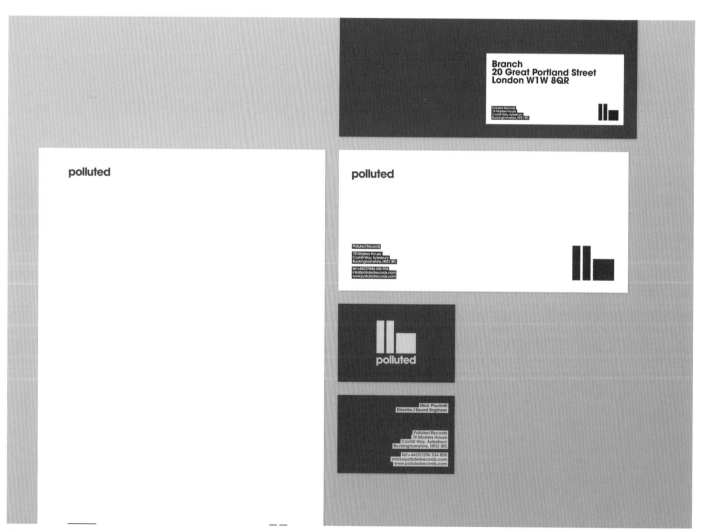

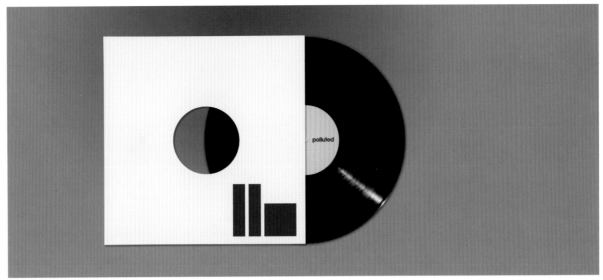

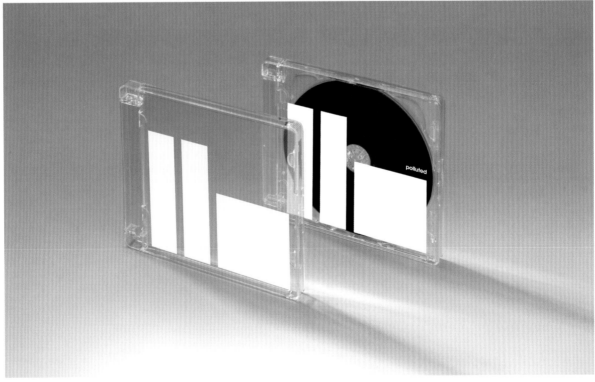

The Private Space

DESIGN: LO SIENTO

The identity for The Private Space was based on the idea of space. Lo Siento created an abstract form from the shape of the brand's name. The Private Space is a meeting point for art and design lovers. It is made up of more than 400 square meters with an exhibition gallery, a shop, a cafe, an editorial label, and last generation printing. The Private Space is a space for literature, photography, music, illustration, fashion, design, and audiovisual media.

THE PRIVATE SPACE GARDEN

THE PRIVATE SPACE SHOP

THE PRIVATE SPACE GALLERY

THE PRIVATE SPACE PRINTS

THE PRIVATE SPACE BOOKS

THE PRIVATE SPACE CAFE

THE PRIVATE SPACE

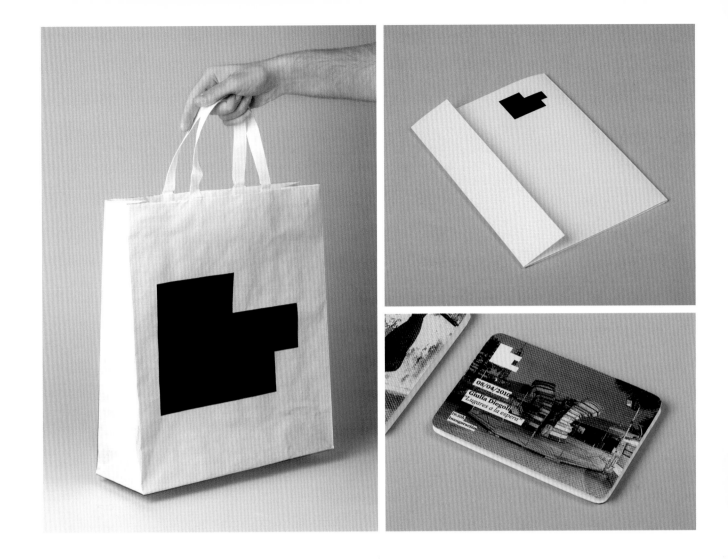

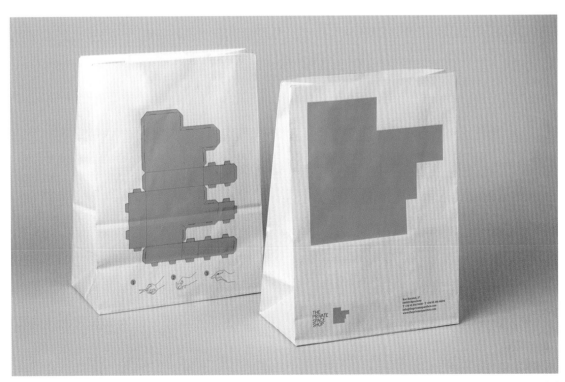

KiD
C

Kid

AGENCY: BERG
DESIGN: DANIEL FREYTAG

BERG was invited by their friends at Made by Wolf (madebywolf.com) to produce a number of T-shirt designs for their new children's fashion label.

They started by creating two designs that work as a set. The idea is that every child may be represented by a letter in the alphabet. The first shirt is kid 'a,' the second kid 'b,' and so forth. The shape of a bear's head frames the letters, creating a simple and dynamic design.

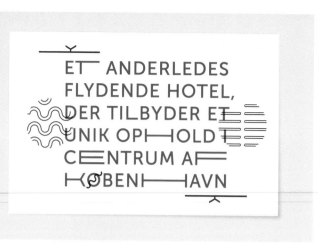

Flydende Hotel

DESIGN: JOSHUA GAJOWNIK

Joshua Gajownik proposed a brand update for a floating hotel in Denmark. The basic pattern was taken from the boat itself and was used to create increasingly intricate supporting designs.

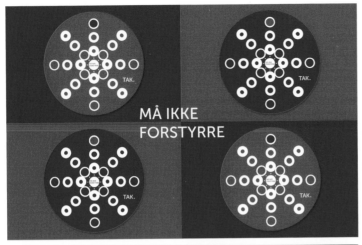
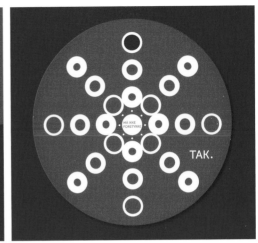

MÅ IKKE
FORSTYRRE

DOOR HATCHES

FACES ON BOAT

ROWERS

FLAG

 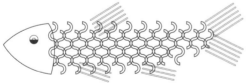    

FISH

FISH TAIL OUT OF WATER

RAILINGS

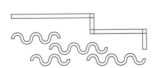 

BENCH WITH A VIEW

LOOKING THROUGH HATCHES

NO SEASICKNESS

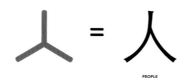

人 = 人

PEOPLE

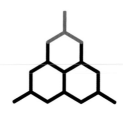

CHAIN REACTION
BRANCHING OUT FROM A SINGLE POINT

The Chain Reaction Project

AGENCY: BRAVO COMPANY
CREATIVE DIRECTION: EDWIN TAN
ART DIRECTION: AMANDA HO
DESIGN: PHARAON SIRAJ

The Chain Reaction Project (TCRP) is a non-profit organization founded in 2009 to help change lives in some of the world's least-developed nations. TCRP's mission is to find a cause and have an effect, thereby inspiring others to be catalysts for change as well. Bravo Company created a series of icons with the logo mark for their various causes. Their card creates its own chain reaction since it can be passed on to 3 other people.

human rights

medical access

mountaineering

charity

hiking

environment

cycling

war-related aid

sustainable energy

animal rights

nature

disaster relief

scientific research

education

logistics

the arts

infrastructure

disability

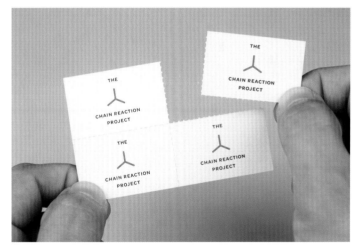

Dresses2Kill

DESIGN: LA LONJA GRÁFICA

Dresses2Kill asked La Lonja Gráfica for a logo that would reflect the spirit of their young and creative made to order clothing and accessories.

To highlight their craftsmanship and love of dressmaking, the team used a graphic language in both the logo and patterns inspired by the weaves of fabrics. Individual threads are represented as simple geometric shapes that take on the look of embroidery.

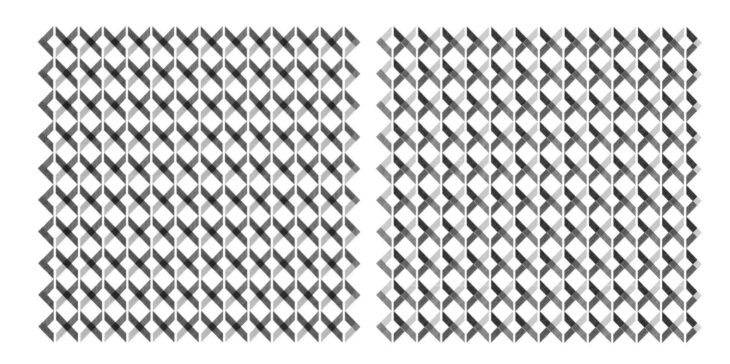

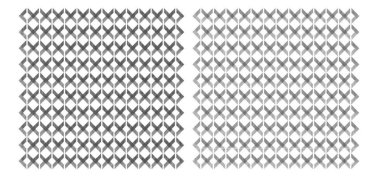

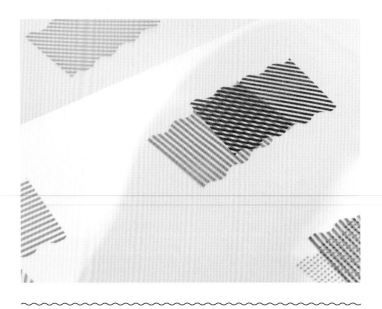

~~~~~~~~~~~~~~~~~~~~~~~~~~~

Liber Skaena

~~~~~~~~~~~~~~~~~~~~~~~~~~~

DESIGN: ROMUALDO FAURA
PHOTOGRPHY: ALFONSO ACEDO

Skaena Liber is an experimental theater company. The identity was based on theater curtains.

There is a main symbol used for common issues, such as stationery, and seven symbols with different textures, representing each genre. These symbols are used and combined depending on the genres of the plays.

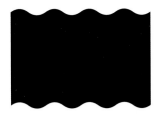

-Liber Skaena

Experimentos Teatrales

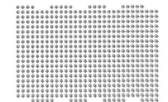

-Liber Skaena

Experimentos Teatrales

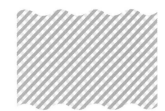

-Liber Skaena

Experimentos Teatrales

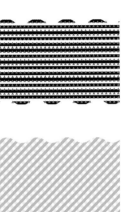 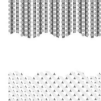 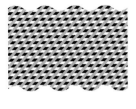 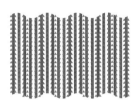

 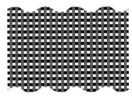  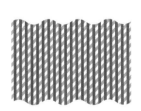

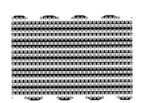  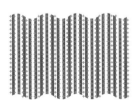 

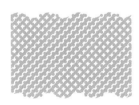 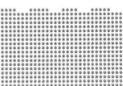  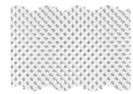

~~~~~~

K2

~~~~~~

DESIGN: SEA DESIGN

Sea Design created the identity and website design for London's leading silkscreen print studio. K2 creates premium work for artists, publishers, and designers.

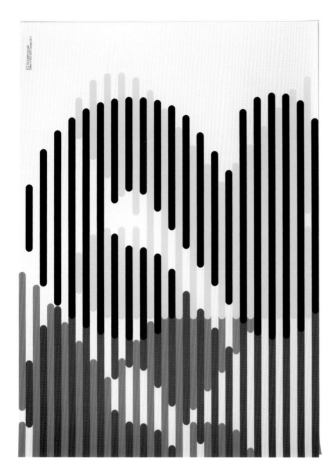

Budapest Corvinus University - Infocommunication Department

DESIGN: MÁRTON HEGEDŰS, KRISTÓF KŐMÍVES

The structure of the emblem is built on the principle of lenticular printing. This technique makes it possible to take separate images (in this case, the four letters of INFO) and unify them in a single image. The elements that compose the new image can be seen separately or together, as a whole. This optical game dislodges the emblem from the static of graphic images and makes it interactive. A pattern consisting of the basic parts of the logo can be seen throughout the identity.

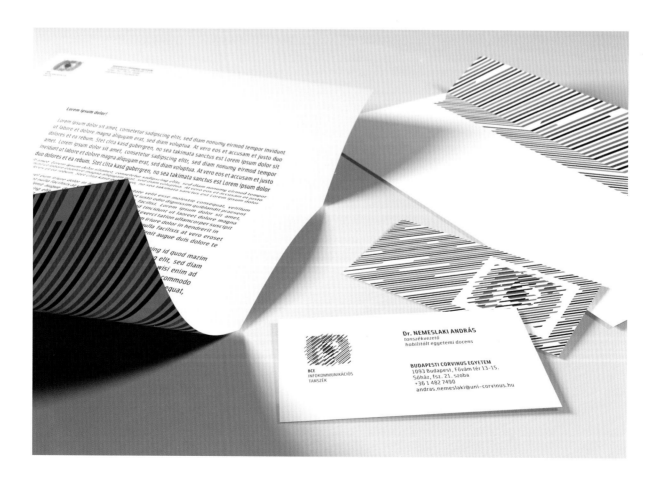

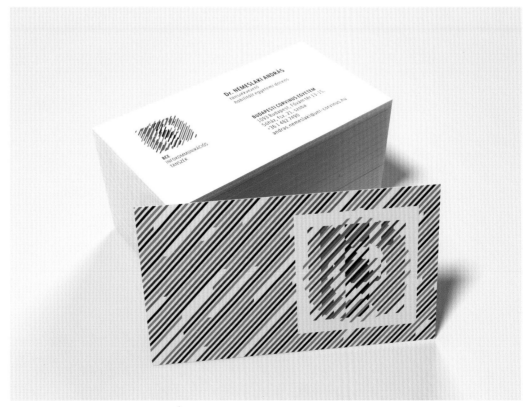

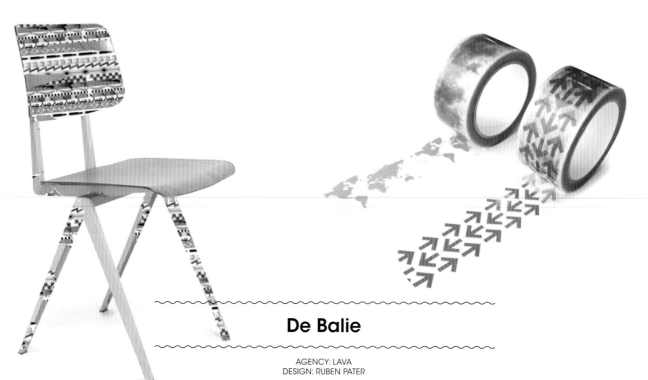

De Balie

AGENCY: LAVA
DESIGN: RUBEN PATER

De Balie is a center for culture and politics that hosts debates, seminars, theater, and films, aimed at current cultural, political, and social issues. De Balie asked Lava to develop its identity, while maintaining its existing logo in Helvetica.

The goal of the re-branding was to clearly position De Balie as a political/cultural meeting place and to create a less high-brow image. De Balie highlights important issues in society: Lava took this fact as a starting point and translated it into an identity where De Balie literally underlines what is important.

For each topic Lava designs a style of underlining that connects to the content. De Balie's logo is underlined in various ways depending on the occasion. This ensures an endless collection of dynamic images while creating a very unified and recognizable identity.

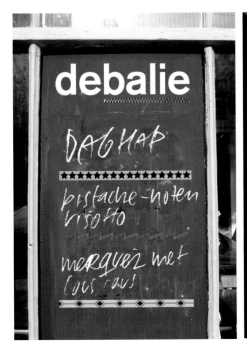

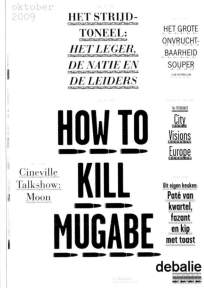

Himalayas Art Museum

DESIGN: LI QI

Himalayas Art Museum is like a huge box full of colorful elements that are various yet unified.

The logos represent the easygoing, young, communicative, comprehensive, collective, and emanative nature of Himalayas Art Museum. The designer wanted other people to be able to add additional graphics to the format, so the public is invited to join in the process of designing the visual identity of the art museum.

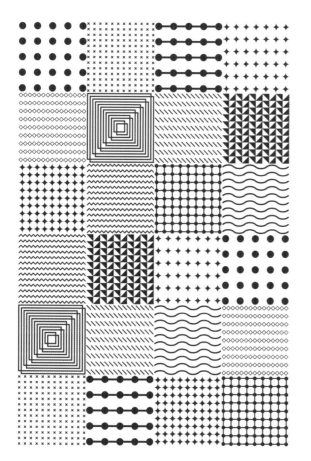

HIMALAYAS ART MUSEUM
• 喜 馬 拉 雅 美 術 館 •

HIMALAYAS ART MUSEUM
• 喜 馬 拉 雅 美 術 館 •

HIMALAYAS ART MUSEUM
• 喜 馬 拉 雅 美 術 館 •

HIMALAYAS ART MUSEUM
• 喜 馬 拉 雅 美 術 館 •

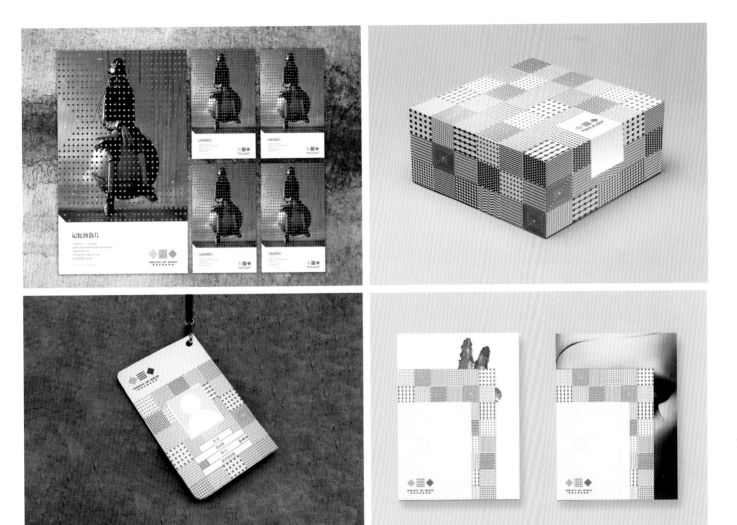

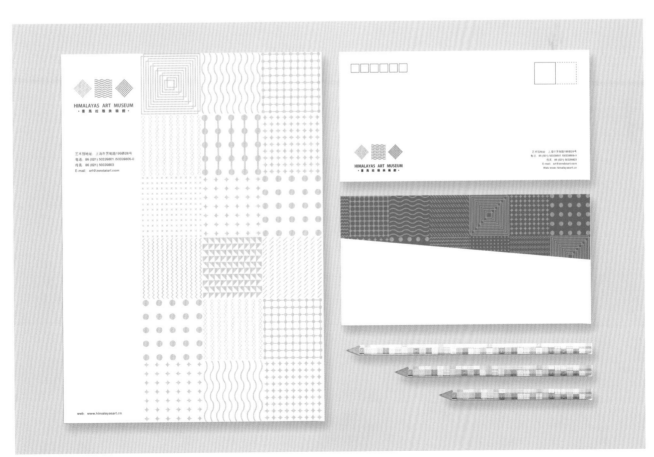

Benetton (Design Proposal)

AGENCY: FABRICA
CREATIVE DIRECTION: OMAR.VULPINARI
DESIGN: GRANT-RU LI

Grant-ru Li started with the concept of a unified design made up of symbols from six different languages. By repeating these symbols, he created an imitation of the Fair Isle pattern. Different languages have different textures. The combination of western and eastern languages creates a rhythm and texture made up of text. Through its use and integration of diverse languages, the design becomes a representation of cultural integration.

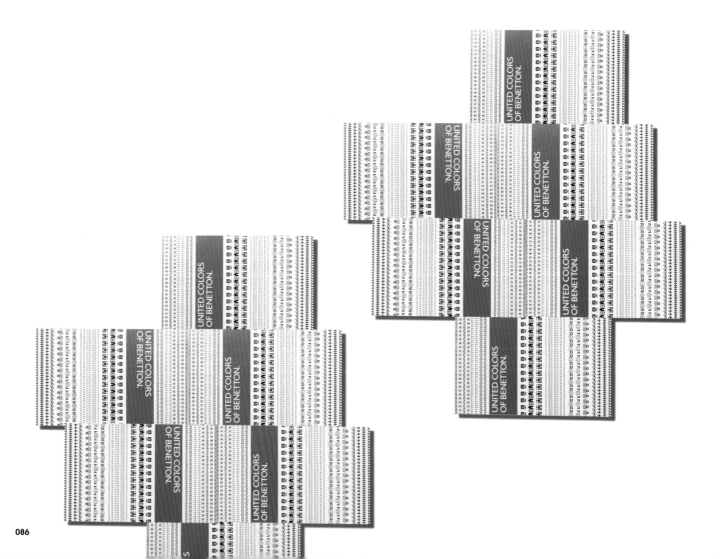

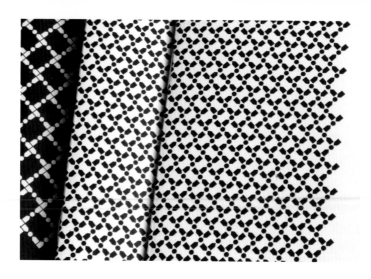

Convention Bureau della Riviera di Rimini

AGENCY: RELÉ AGENCY - STUDIO TASSINARI/VETTA
DESIGN: LEONARDO SONNOLI, IRENE BACCHI

The new visual identity for Convention Bureau della Riviera di Rimini visually represents the meetings and interactions the convention bureau facilitates. Both the logo and custom font called "Riviera" were based on the concept of coming together.

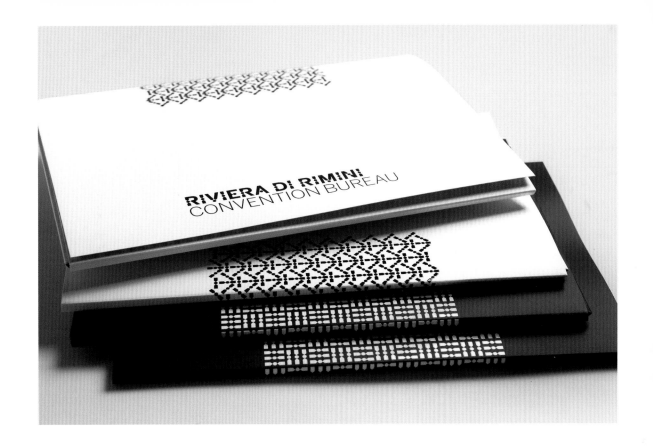

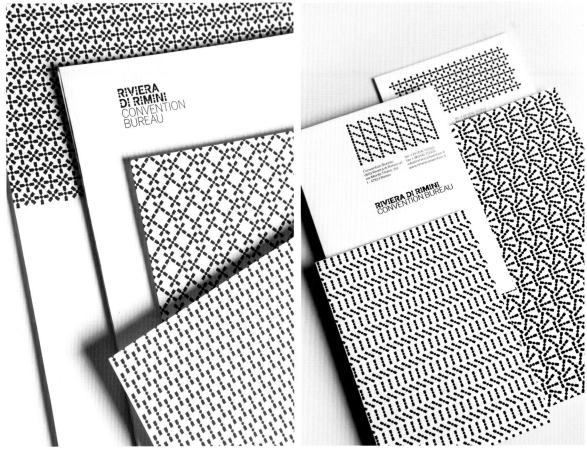

President's Design Award 2009

AGENCY: H55
CREATIVE DIRECTION: HANSON HO
DESIGN: HANSON HO

H55 was selected to do the branding for the President's Design Award, Singapore's highest design accolade which recognises good design in the fields of architecture and urban design, fashion design, industrial and product design, interior design, and visual communication. The team conceptualised the theme 'metamorphosis' for the President's Design Award 2009, and expressed this with the use of a tessellation seen throughout the designs.

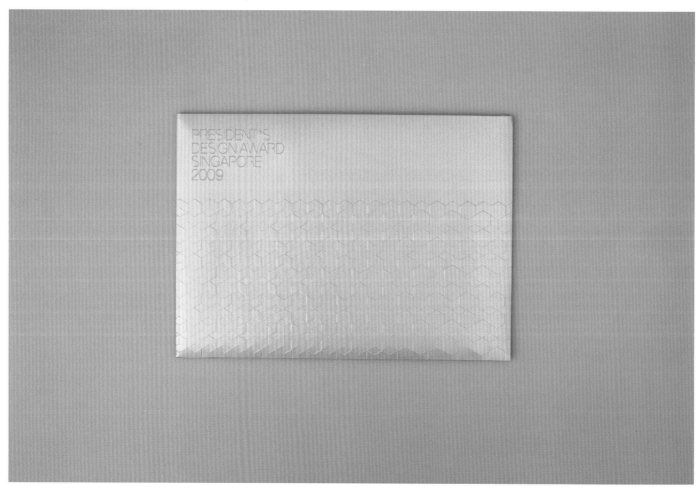

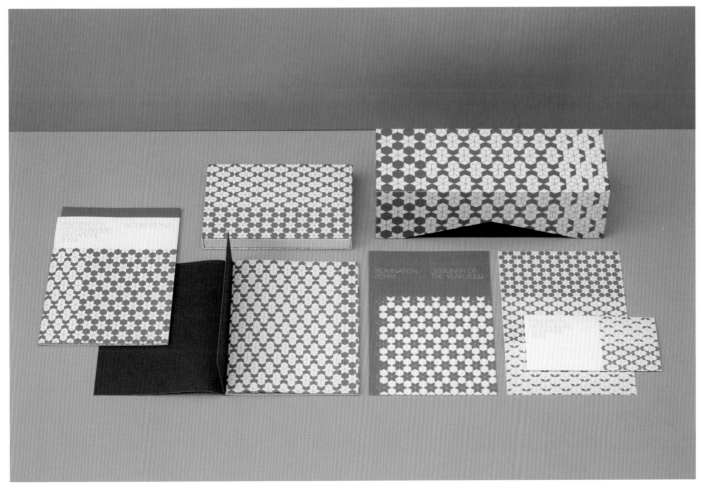

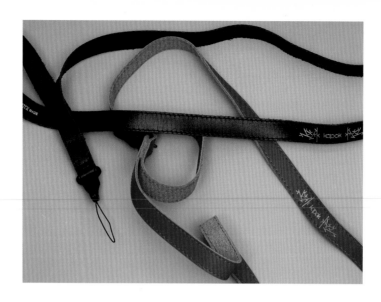

Kapok Identity

AGENCY: H55
CREATIVE DIRECTION: HANSON HO
DESIGN: HANSON HO

Kapok is a design retail store turned café based in Hong Kong.

The identity was inspired by the kapok tree the brand is named after. Using the letter 'k' as a modular unit, H55 created a visual identity that is well-crafted, organic, and always growing to reflect the range of products the store retails.

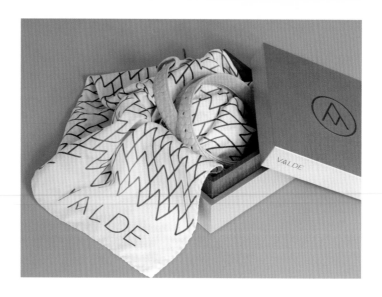

Valde

AGENCY: EDGE DESIGN
CREATIVE DIRECTION: STEVE EDGE
SENIOR DESIGNER: TOM WEST
DESIGNER: NICK DART

Valde's belts are made from fish leather and titanium. The pattern was designed to reference the Tilapia fish's scales as well as the brand's outdoor heritage.

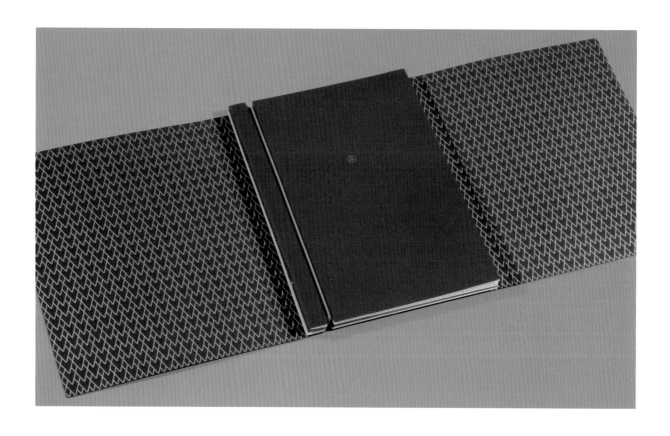

_Ground

AGENCY: HELLOME
ART DIRECTION/DESIGN:TILL WIEDECK

The branding system for the Munich based music label _Ground was inspired by soil layers. The idea of different layers of earth is translated into a visual system by assigning a different handdrawn black and white pattern to each section and artist of the label. So everytime the label signs a new artist or adds a new section, another layer is added to the visual system. This abstractly visualizes the diversity of the label and the complexity of their activities. This system is combined with a clean but remarkable logotype; the underscore in the logo is a symbol for the ground itself.

HelloMe developed a set of printed applications, consisting of stationery, complimentary cards, envelopes, and business cards. All feature a different set of patterns on the back and can be combined to produce a bigger set of layers.

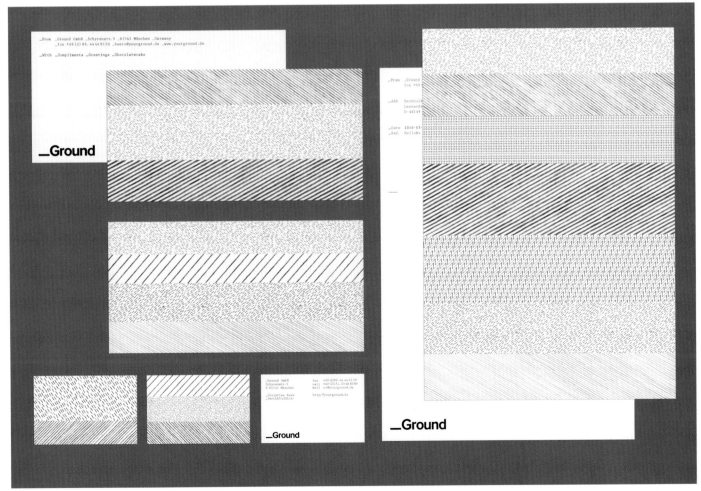

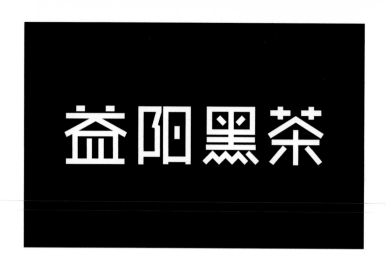

Yiyang Black Tea

AGENCY: RUIYI DESIGN OFFICE
DESIGN: HU CHANGFA

Ruiyi Design Office designed the visual identity for Yiyang Black Tea.

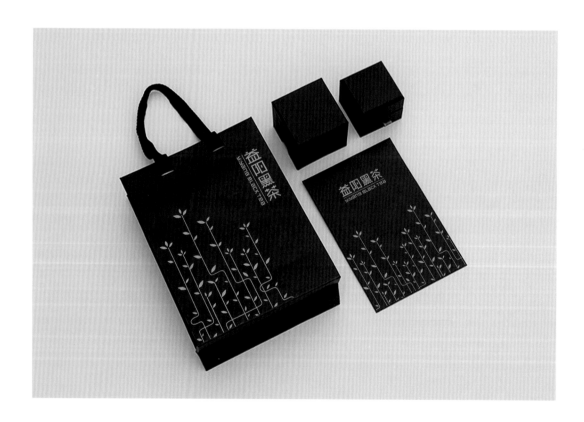

Design Shop oooo.com.ua

AGENCY: GRAPHIC DESIGN STUDIO BY YURKO GUTSULYAK
DESIGN: YURKO GUTSULYAK

Yurko Gutsulyak aimed to create a graphically simple name that was easy to read and remember. Working on the assumption that the way a name looks is more important than the way it sounds, oooo.com.ua was developed. The name has the added benefit of being easy to read in both Roman and Cyrillic fonts as well as graphic language. In the name, the "O's" are objects that represent a variety of exclamations and emotions. Each "O" is also a circle—one of the most fundamental figures of design. One of the main components of the oooo.com.ua identification is an original decorative font designed specifically for this project. The font was named Gerdan as the letters look like decorative beads that emphasize a connection between contemporary design and traditional Ukrainian arts and crafts.

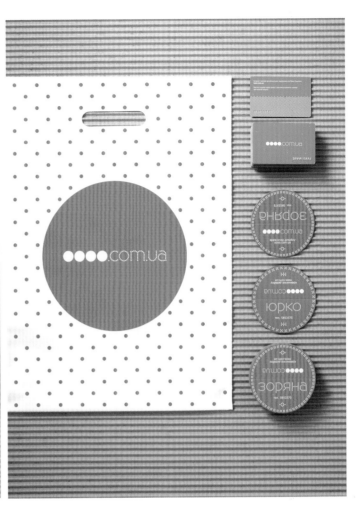

SALSA
MARINERA

25Og

SALSA
PIMIENTA
VERDE

25Og

ATUGUSTO

SALSA
THAI

25Og

ATUGUSTO

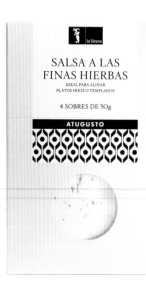

SALSA A LAS
FINAS HIERBAS

IDEAL PARA ALIÑAR
PLATOS FRÍOS O TEMPLADOS

4 SOBRES DE 5Og

ATUGUSTO

SALSA
MARINER

25Og

ATUGUSTO

A tu gusto

AGENCY: MARNICH ASSOCIATES
ART DIRECTION: WLADIMIR MARNICH
DESIGN: GRISELDA MARTÍ
ILLUSTRATION: BO LUNDBERG

Marnich and Associates was asked to develop a brand design for La Sirena's new range of non-frozen products.

SALSA
THAI

25Og

ATUGUSTO

SALSA A LAS
FINAS HIERBAS

IDEAL PARA ALIÑAR
PLATOS FRÍOS O TEMPLADOS

4 SOBRES DE 5Og

ATUGUSTO

SALSA
MARINERA

25Og

ATUGUSTO

SALSA
PIMIENTA
VERDE

25Og

ATUGUSTO

ALLIOLI
SALSA
ROMESCO
ALLIOLI

MAYONESA
220ml

SALSA
COCKTAIL
220ml

NACHOS
APERITIVO SALADO DE MAÍZ
125g

ATUGUSTO

SALSA
MARINERA
250g
ATUGUSTO

SALSA
PIMIENTA VERDE
250g
ATUGUSTO

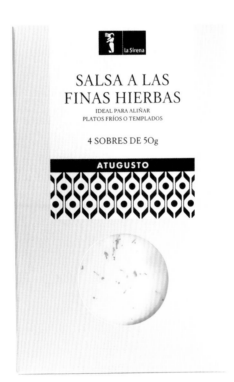

La Sirena

SALSA A LAS FINAS HIERBAS
IDEAL PARA ALIÑAR
PLATOS FRÍOS O TEMPLADOS

4 SOBRES DE 50g

ATUGUSTO

SALSA
BARBACOA
4 TARRINAS DE 50g
ATUGUSTO

SALSA PARA
REDONDOS DE
POLLO ASADOS
250g
ATUGUSTO

SALSA
THAI
250g
ATUGUSTO

SALSA
TEX-MEX
4 TARRINAS DE 50g
ATUGUSTO

Point G Plaisirs Gourmands

AGENCY: CHEZ VALOIS
DESIGN: MICHEL VALOIS
PHOTOGRAPHY: SYLVIE RACICOT

The founders of Point G wanted to create an identity that they could relate to. Even though they are considered the masters of macarons and other gourmet delights in Montreal, they did not want to play up that reputation. In this respect, the cliché of elitist luxury that some pastry brands project is a million miles away from who Point G truly is. Because they had, some years before, come up with the irreverent idea of naming their Company Point G for Point Gourmet. Chez Valois wanted to assume that identity and express it fully. The result of the packaging platform is powerful, while speaking with finesse and humour. The big words are now part of the vocabulary of the brand, and express themselves without vulgarity, surfing the subtlety and sensuality of a culinary and sensory vocabulary.

Custom Color Corp

DESIGN: DESIGN RANCH

Custom Color Corp is a large format digital printer that takes pride in taking every project to the extreme. Whether it's stadiums or bus wraps, if you can think it, they can ink it. Design Ranch took the hint and designed a bold new brand inspired by the process of printing. Ink inspired everything from the eye-catching photos, to the CMYK graphic elements. At Custom Color Corp, they ink outside the box.

CUSTOMER SERVICE

th**ink** fast.

Custom Color provides you with the service you
deserve. Our experienced staff will work with you
to meet your deadline in the most economical way
possible, without compromising on quality. With
an average job turnaround of only 2 days, you're
inked in a blink.

custom color corp

p. 816.595.6800 f. 816.595.6801 w. www.customcolor.com 1. 2850 burlington street north kc mo. 64116

custom color corp
think big · think fast · think printing

custom color corp

Line-one Chain Restaurant

AGENCY: VBN

Line-one has achieved a harmonic relationship with the city and its customers through its innovative approach.

The two yellow lines in the design connect the shop to the road and surrounding area. The result is both unique and effective. The geometric zebra pattern creates a dynamic visual effect that reflects Line-one's goal to "entertain through innovation."

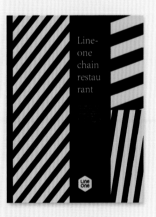

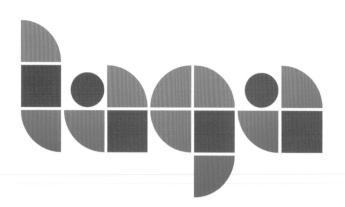

~~~~~~

Laga

~~~~~~

DESIGN: JIYOUNG LEE

Laga is an industrial design firm that has merged with Desgrippes Grobe, a well-known branding company. The two became Brandimage. Jiyoung Lee designed Laga's identity in order to separate and emphasize it and its concept work.

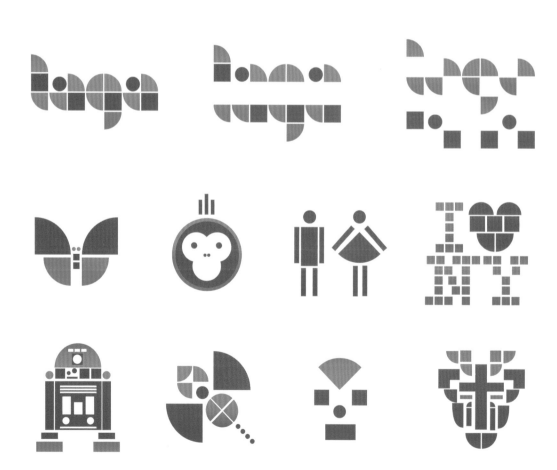

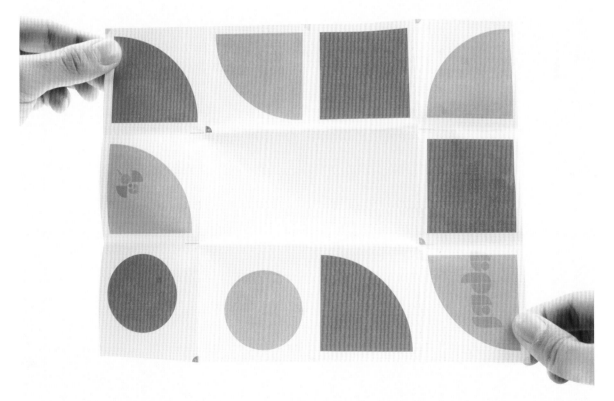

Zeri Crafts

AGENCY: MAYÚSCULA BRANDS
DESIGN DIRECTION: ROCÍO MARTINAVARRO
DESIGN: ROCÍO MARTINAVARRO, LUCIA PIGLIAPOCHI

Zeri Crafts is a company that aims to reinterpret the richness of the Gulf handicrafts with its homewares. The name refers to the fine gold thread that embellishes the region's typical gowns. The visual identity presents gold motifs inspired by Sadu Bedouin weaving in a new and delicate way reminiscent of woven zeri threads. The identity consists of modular designs made up of half-square triangles. Special care was put in the typography to achieve equal visual weight in the Latin and Arabic logotypes.

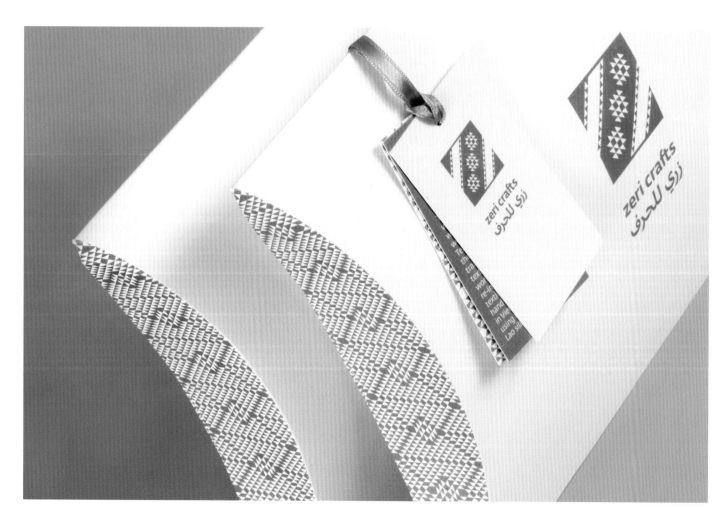

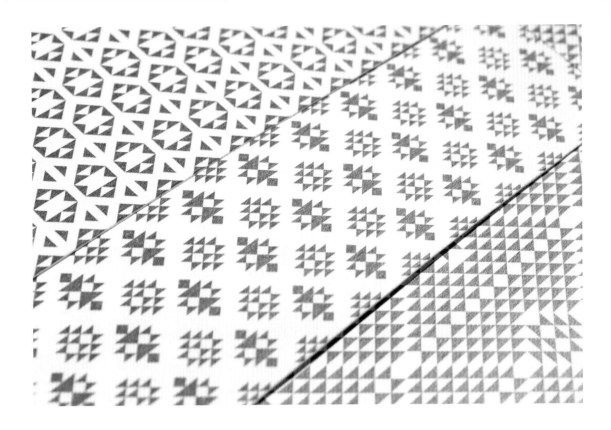

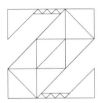

 zeri crafts
زري للحرف

 zeri crafts
زري للحرف

 zeri crafts
زري للحرف

**Lento leeento.
Sin prisas.
Así es el proceso
de elaboración del**

PanPan Bakery

AGENCY: MAYÚSCULA BRANDS
CREATIVE DIRECTION: ROCÍO MARTINAVARRO
DESIGN: ROCÍO MARTINAVARRO

Mayúscula Brands designed the visual identity for PanPan, an artisan bakery chain in Valencia.

The pattern is a contemporary reinterpretation of the traditional ear of wheat, and thus represents the basic ingredient of bread and is easily recognizable. The chevron pattern is also reminiscent of the artisan esparto baskets used to display the bread and the modified opus spicatum found in the interiors of the bakeries.

The naming concept is based on word repetition in order to emphasize authenticity. Bread-bread, as in real bread. This system is carried throughout all communication materials and has endless possibilities, all grouped under one slogan with a double meaning: "PanPan. Repetirás" (BreadBread. You will repeat).

Custom typography was used for the logotype.

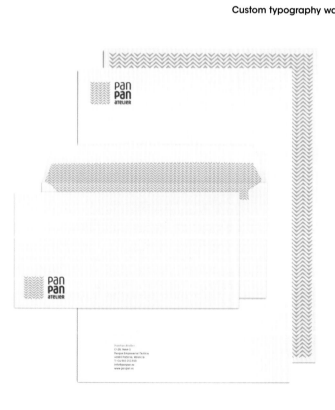

Crujiente crujiente, porque cuidamos todos los detalles del horneado para obtener una corteza espectacular.
PanPan. Repetirás

Devórame otra vez.
Devórame otra vez.
PanPan. Repetirás

Lento leeem...
Sin prisas.
Así es el proceso de elaboración del auténtico pan.
PANPAN. Repetirás

pan
pan
ATELIER®

~~~~~~

Haiti

~~~~~~

AGENCY: SVIDESIGN
DESIGN: SASHA VIDAKOVIC

These posters were donated to raise funds after the earthquake disaster. Rather than focusing on the victims of the earthquake, the strong zig-zag pattern is used to depict the vibrations that caused the disaster, as well as the vastness of the ocean and the island of Haiti in the middle of it.

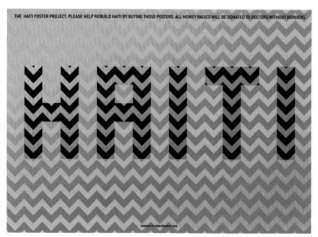

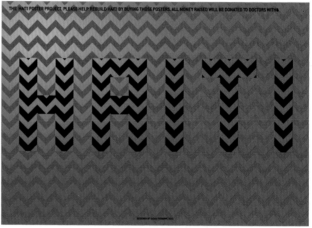

POOLTRADESHOW

AGENCY: HYPE TYPE STUDIO
DESIGN: PAUL HUTCHISON

Paul Hutchison was in charge of the event style and design and art direction. He designed the brochures, invitations, bags, and T-shirts.

POOLTRADESHOW is the leading art and design driven fashion trade show for emerging brands. Retail visionaries come to scout hot new items designed specifically for the boutique market. From emerging designers to the worlds best graphic artists, POOL is where art and design meet and shape the trends. The show earns its industry reputation as a launching pad for emerging art and design driven brands that quickly become industry household names. The design direction for the August 2011 Show was developed using a number of patterns, reflecting exciting new directions in fashion.

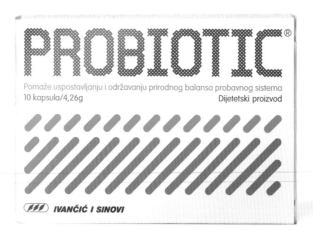

~~~~~~

Ivancic i Sinovi

~~~~~~

AGENCY: SVIDESIGN
DESIGN: SASHA VIDAKOVIC, IAN MIZON, ZANETA DRGOVA

SVIDesign designed the packaging for a pharmaceutical company that produces high quality diet and food supplements.

The design concept drew on notions of family values, traditional recipes, and the sense of comfort they provide. Embroidery-inspired patterns are used to conceptually and visually unify the whole product family. They provided a base for the construction of bespoke font used for product names. Beyond these strong and recognizable forms, bright colours are introduced to enhance the personality of each product as well as the product line in general.

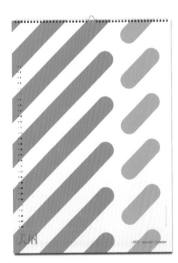

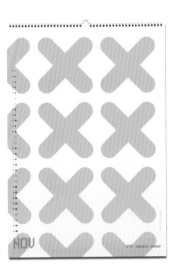

~~~~~~

Mobile Mate

~~~~~~

AGENCY: OXNU DESIGN
DESIGN: MR. RABBIT
ILLUSTRATION: TYSON TSE

With the increasingly fierce competition in the mobile industry, Mobile Mate invited OXNU Design to design new visual identities that would better relate to their growing youth audience.

The team's concept was to simplify the logo itself and use the shape of the letter "M" to create a wide variety of graphics and patterns in order to reflect the vitality and creativity of the Company of Mobile Mate and provide strong memorable identities to the target audience.

MOBILE MATE.

MOBILE MATE.

MOBILE MATE.

p (+61) 7 334 421 90   e:mobilemate@hotmail.com
shop 72a, sunnybank plaza, mains road, qld 4109

Mohawk

AGENCY: PENTAGRAM
ART DIRECTOR: MICHAEL BIERUT
DESIGN: MICHAEL BIERUT, KATIE BARCELONA, JOE MARIANEK

Mohawk, a family business founded in 1931, is North America's largest privately owned manufacturer of fine papers and envelopes. Pentagram helped to reinvent Mohawk for the digital world.

The new mark is based on the letter M. The logo serves as a monogram for the name Mohawk, but is also inspired by the papermaking process and the printmaking process, both of which involve paper moving around cylinders. The forms of the logo suggest paper rolls, printing presses, and circuit boards, as well as the ideas of connection and communication, the core functions of paper. "Whether it's for a small book of family photos or a brochure for a giant corporation, it's all about communication," says Bierut. Applied to advertising, swatchbooks, brochures, and ream wraps, the logo is a building block in a flexible branding system that includes more than a dozen color variations and countless patterns based on the mark.

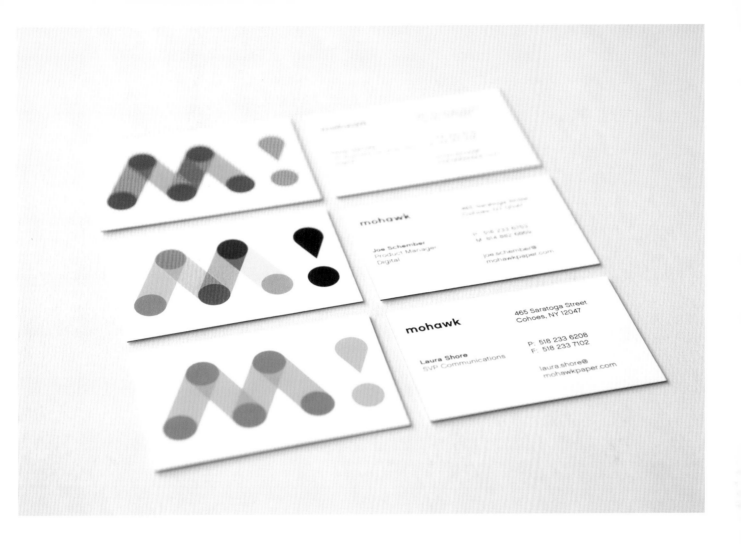

mohawk

Joe Schember
Product Manager
Digital

465 Saratoga Street
Cohoes, NY 12047

P: 518 233 6753
M: 614 882 6864

joe.schember@
mohawkpaper.com

mohawk

Laura Shore
SVP Communications

465 Saratoga Street
Cohoes, NY 12047

P: 518 233 6208
F: 518 233 7102

laura.shore@
mohawkpaper.com

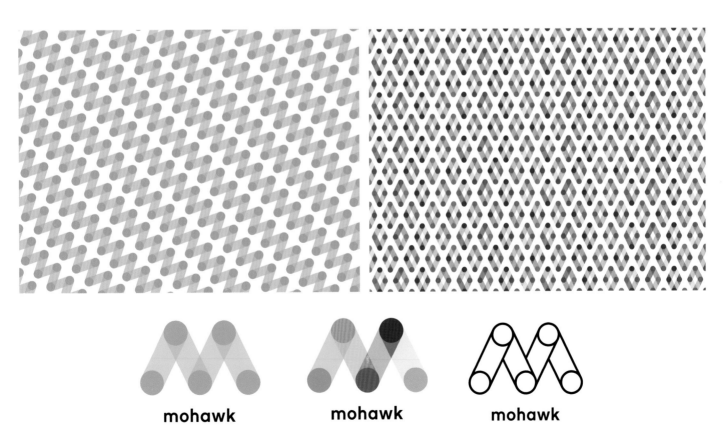

mohawk   mohawk   mohawk

China Poblano Restaurant

AGENCY: TOORMIX
DESIGN: ORIOL ARMENGOU, FERRAN MITJANS
INTERIOR DESIGN: SEED DESIGN
PHOTOGRAPHY: THOMAS SCHAUER(PRODUCT), JEFF GREEN(INTERIOR)

China Poblano is a Mexican and Chinese restaurant located in Cosmopolitan Hotel Las Vegas and directed by chef José Andrés. The identity design plays with the iconography of both cultures and Toormix has developed different graphics for the restaurant: menus, cards, napkins, stickers, etc., as well as some elements of the façade and interior of the restaurant.

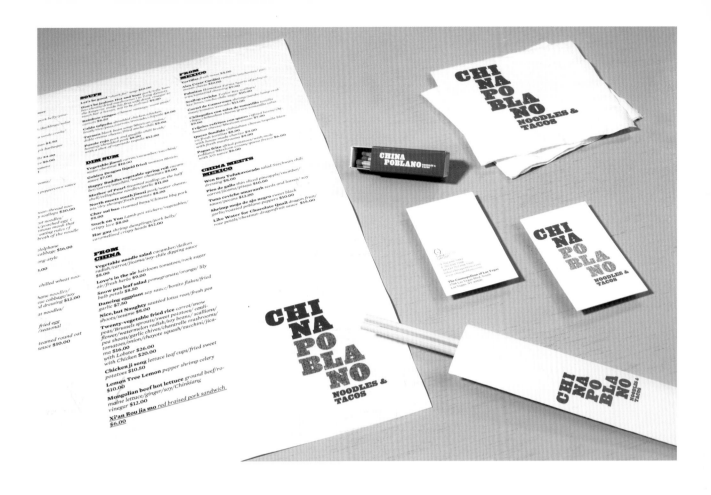

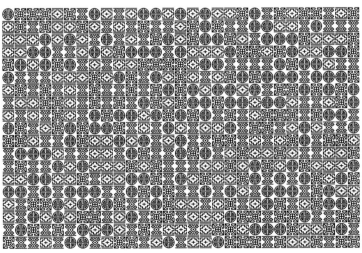

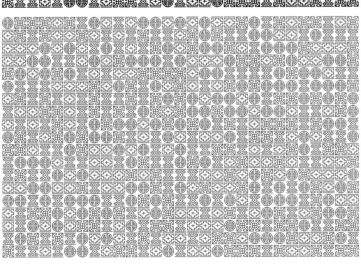

CHI NA PO BLA NO

BY JOSÉ ANDRÉS

Stix

AGENCY: STUDIO EGREGIUS
ART DIRECTION: LE HUY ANH
DESIGN: LE HUY ANH, VU TUAN AN, DOAN THANH QUYNH

Stix, a fine-dining establishment in the heart of Saigon, brings the gourmet taste and style of Vietnamese cuisine to both local and foreign clients. Studio Egregius' work ranged from brand story-telling to complete design development.

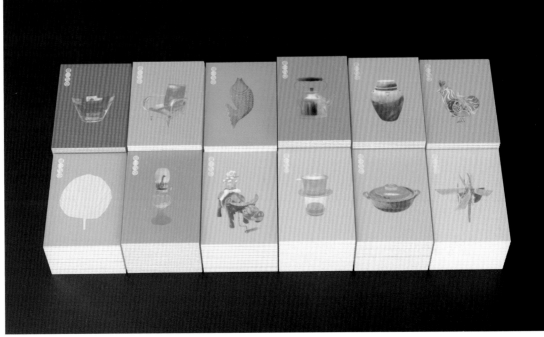

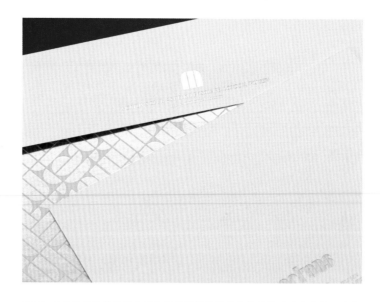

Mortons Private Members Club

AGENCY: EDGE DESIGN
CREATIVE DIRECTION: STEVE EDGE
SENIOR DESIGNER: TOM WEST

The Mortons Private Members Club identity was created to reflect the diverse mix of clientele that make up the clubs unique membership. The pattern was used across all collateral using gold inks and foils.

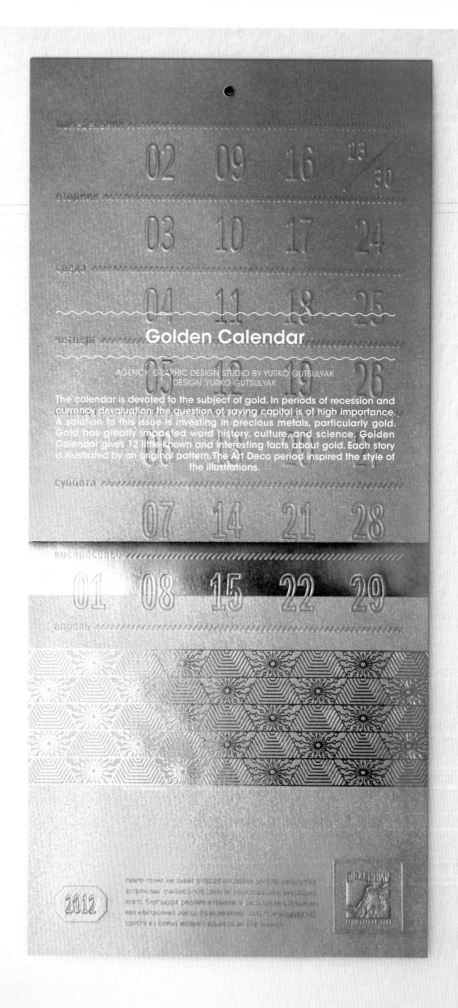

Golden Calendar

AGENCY: GRAPHIC DESIGN STUDIO BY YURKO GUTSULYAK
DESIGN: YURKO GUTSULYAK

The calendar is devoted to the subject of gold. In periods of recession and currency devaluation, the question of saving capital is of high importance. A solution to this issue is investing in precious metals, particularly gold. Gold has greatly impacted word history, culture, and science. Golden Calendar gives 12 little-known and interesting facts about gold. Each story is illustrated by an original pattern. The Art Deco period inspired the style of the illustrations.

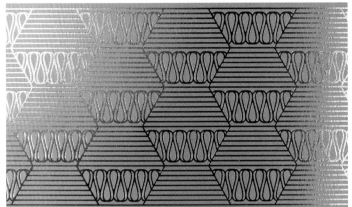

~~~~~~

Duck Duck Goose

~~~~~~

AGENCY: GARDENS&CO.
CREATIVE DIRECTION: WILSON TANG
DESIGN: JEFFREY TAM, WONG KIN CHUNG

gardens&co. was asked to develop a new logo and visual identity for the European furniture company Duck Duck Goose. A unique typeface and visual language were created to represent the Art-Deco style of the furniture. The re-branding project included stationery, a product brochure (a set of postcards), in-store posters, a swing tag, and a product label.

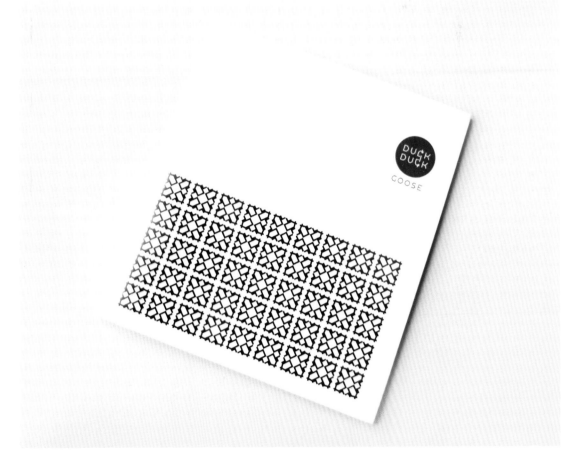

~~~~~~

Camerata de Lausanne

~~~~~~

ART DIRECTION: DEMIAN CONRAD
SCRIPT AND GENERATOR: MATHIEU RUDAZ, QWERTZ

Demian Conrad's research led him to the work of Ernst Chladni, a German physicist and the father of modern acoustics. Chladni had discovered that by taking a copper disc sprinkled with sand and rubbing it with a bow, he could generate geometrical figures. This fact demonstrates that music also has a physical effect on matter. Demian followed the geometrical thread discovered by Chladni and used it on all communication media for Camerata de Lausanne. To give it a more contemporary feel and make it more manageable, Mathieu Rudaz wrote software that would allow them to generate images directly on a computer using a specific frequency.

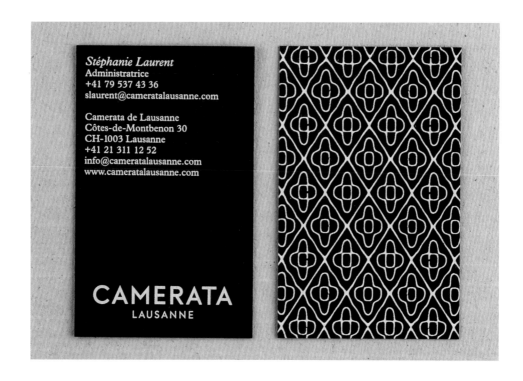

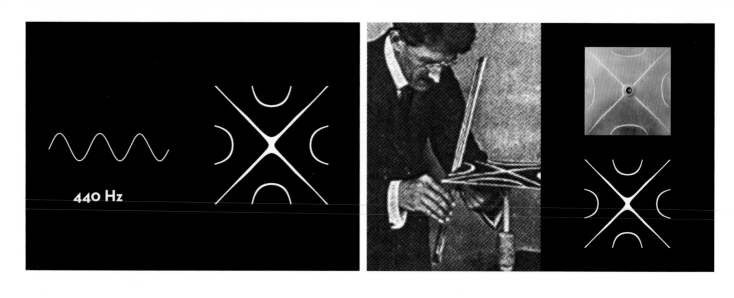

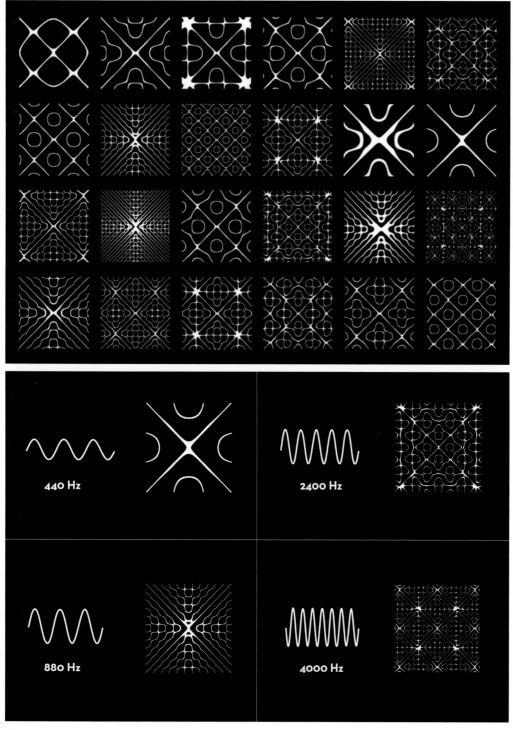

440 Hz

440 Hz

2400 Hz

880 Hz

4000 Hz

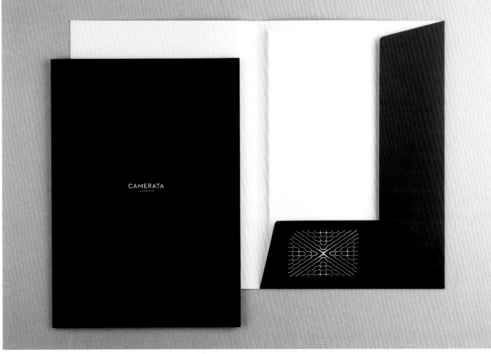

~~~~~~

Gabbani

~~~~~~

DESIGN: DEMIAN CONRAD
PHOTOGRAPHY: OLIVIER LOVEY, SYLVAIN MELTZ

Gabbani is the oldest delicatessen in the Swiss Italian region (1937). It is an old family business that survived and flourished until it became a symbol of state-of-the-art food and food preparation in the food industry. 30 people work to serve their customers the best possible products. The company is divided into the following sectors: food (vegetables, fruits, meet, wine and spirits, flowers, bread, pasta, and G product line), restaurant, bed & breakfast, and catering.

Demian Conrad created Gabanni's new identity and designed a few of their promotional campaigns.

The aim of the project was to create a fashionable and bold identity in order to make Gabbani stand out from the crowd in a competitive market. The designs visually reference the flavour of the 30s, have a mix of various typographies, and use the black & white optical art typical of the 60s.

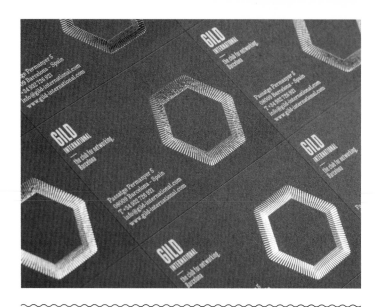

~~~~~~~~~~~~~~~~~~~~~~~~~~~~~~~~~~~~~~~

Gild

~~~~~~~~~~~~~~~~~~~~~~~~~~~~~~~~~~~~~~~

DESIGN: MUCHO

Gild hired Mucho to help establish them as the premier international club for networking in Barcelona. The team decided to add "international" to the logo and create the baseline "the club for networking in Barcelona." The hexagon is an omnipresent shape in the architecture of Barcelona and represents the city and networking. The club's headquarters is its heart. Its symbol and values are always present in a subtle and elegant way. In order to demonstrate the space and the values they designed a set of icons that represent the institution.

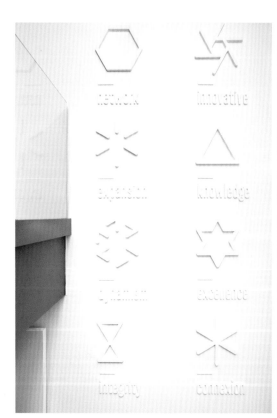

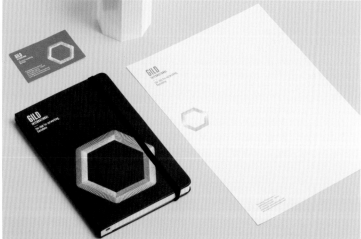

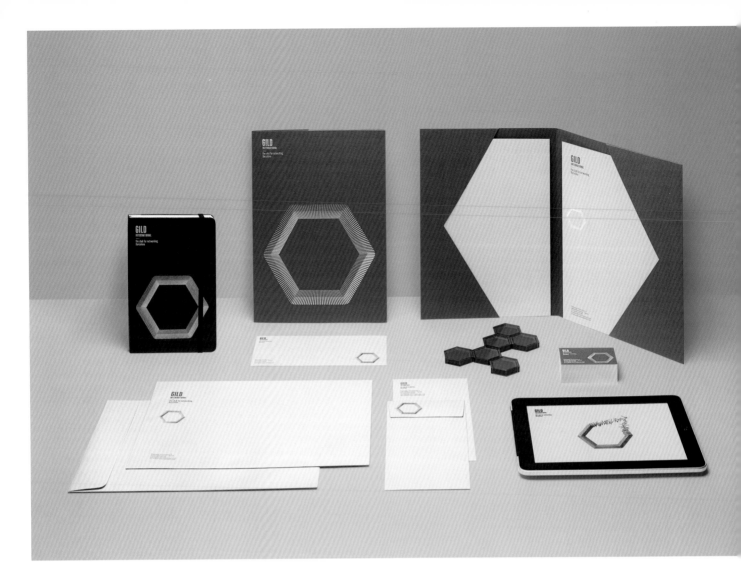

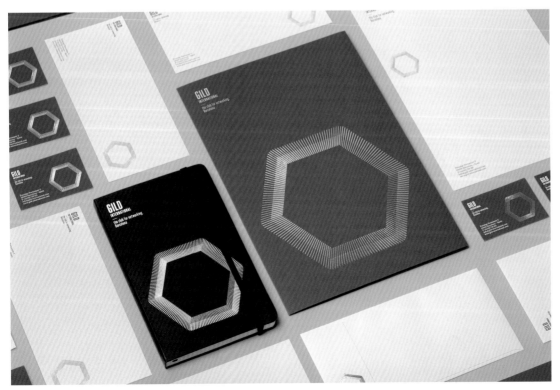

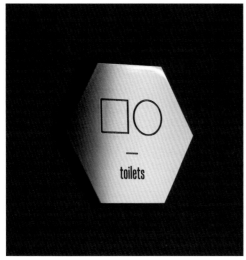

The Sheffield Honey Company

AGENCY: DED ASSOCIATES
DESIGN: NIK DAUGHTRY, JON DAUGHTRY, ROB BARBER

The Sheffield Honey Company is an artisan producer of premium quality local English honey and the finest beeswax products.

DED was tasked with creating a new identity that would stand out from and stay clear of the sticky stereotypes associated with honey brands, including bees. It was vital that the identity communicate Sheffield's industrial heritage, whilst referencing the artisans attention to detail when it came to their premium quality honey.

DED's approach was to create a utilitarian logo/brand solution that would allow the products' natural colors to take center stage. An overtly minimal typographic treatment was used, synonymous with the functionality of the steel factories of the city's past. The label pays a subtle homage to the old street trams and bus tickets that would get clipped by the conductor on presentation. The simple line mark is the joining of a honey drop and the hexagonal form of a steel nut.

.SE

AGENCY: BEDOW
DESIGN: PERNICLAS BEDOW
ILLUSTRATION: PERNICLAS BEDOW

.SE, the foundation responsible for the Swedish top-level domain, arranged One Million Domain Names to celebrate the millionth .SE domain. Bedow designed the identity for the event. The assignment included units such as invitations, posters, T-shirts, and beer labels.

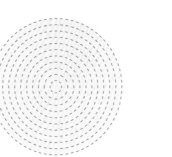

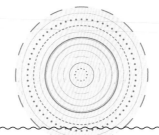
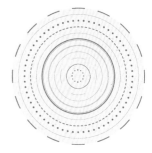

Other Press Publishing Company

DESIGN: KAYLA JANG

The "O" logo for Other Press Publishing Company changes to match each book's specific genre.

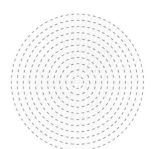

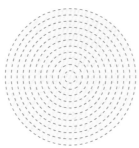

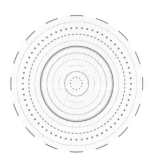

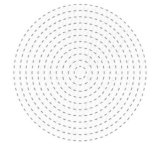

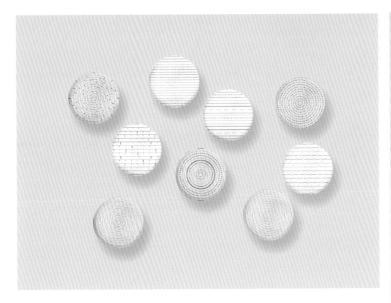

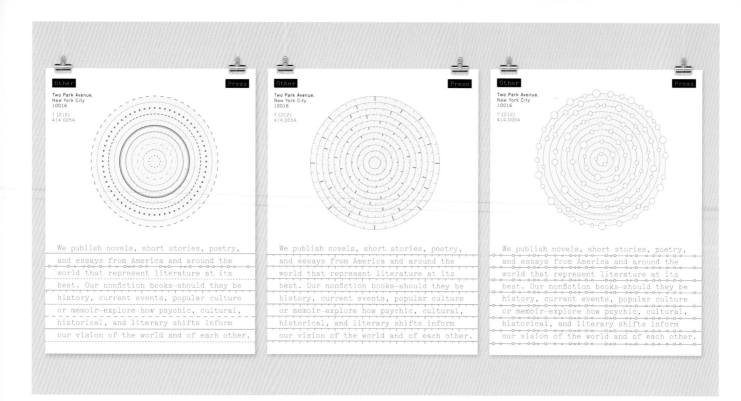

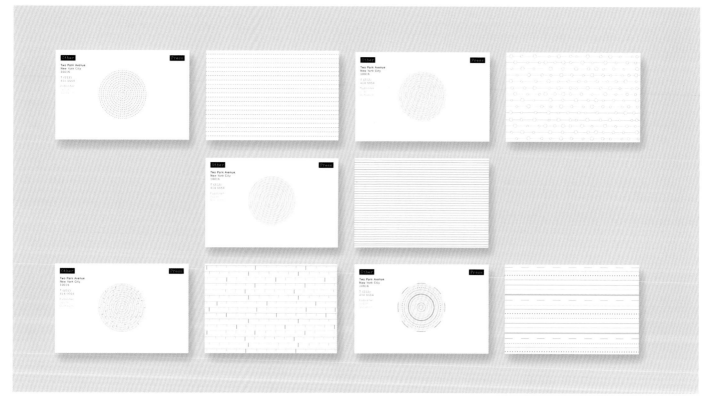

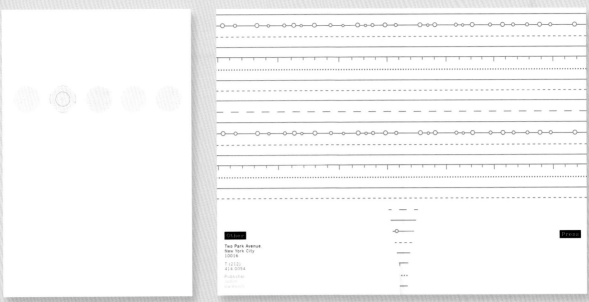

Les Tartes de Françoise

AGENCY: CODEFRISKO
DESIGN: AUDREY SCHAYES, THOMAS WYNGAARD

Tartes de Françoise sells savory pies and delicious cakes in fine groceries. They own 7 different shops and are currently opening several others in Belgium. Their products are also provided in several nice restaurants.

Codefrisko was responsible for the photo shoot direction and designed the new visual identity, the website, stationery, window and display communication, packaging, and more for this well known Belgian bakery.

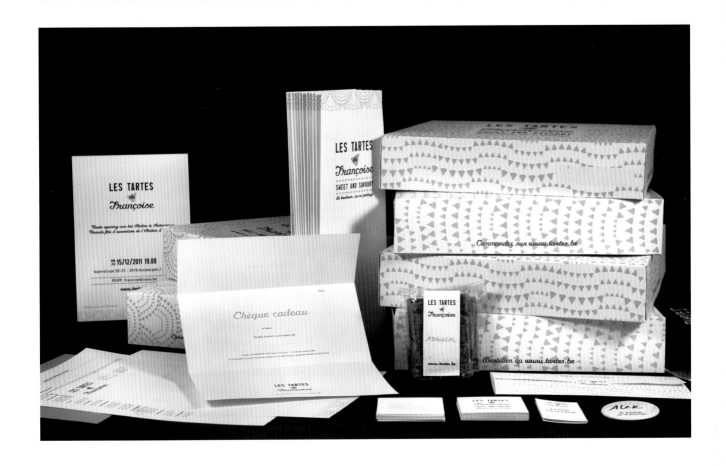

D100

DESIGN: MIND DESIGN

D100 is a modern dentistry at the Barbican (100 Aldersgate street). The identity was inspired by the raking patterns around stones in Japanese Zen gardens and protective layers of enamel around teeth. The patterns have also been applied to the interior around furniture and other various objects.

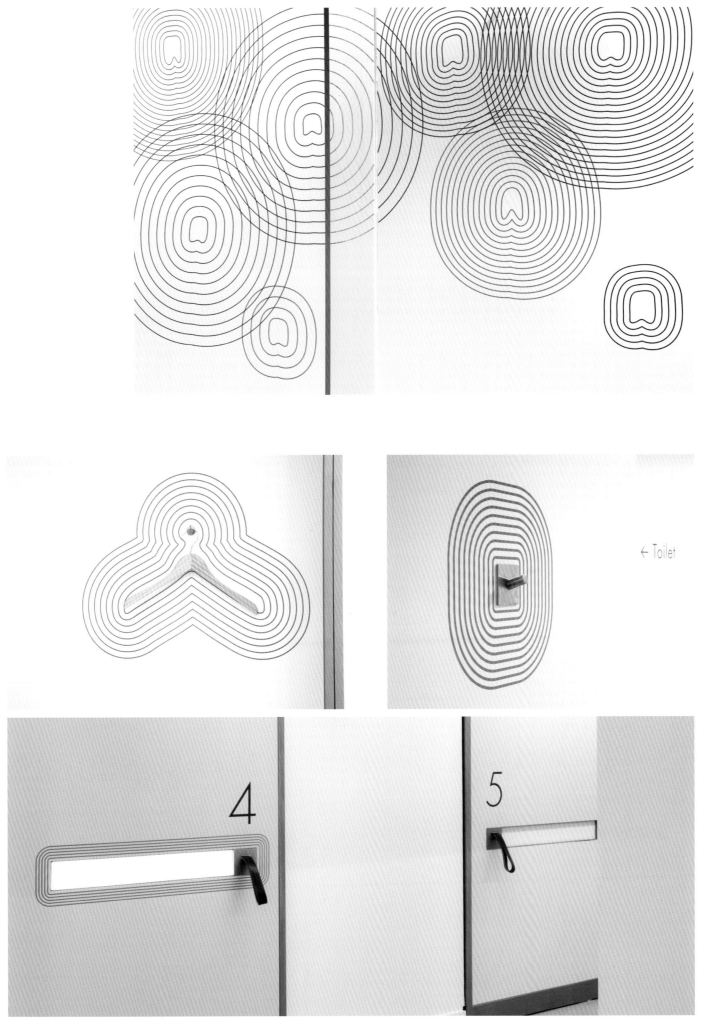

← Toilet

4

5

~~~~~~

360° Shop

~~~~~~

AGENCY: MILKXHAKE
DESIGN DIRECTION: JAVIN MO
DESIGN: JAVIN MO, JAN CHEUNG

Initiated by Sandu Cultural Media in Guangzhou, China, Design 360°shop is a new concept store derived from the design magazine Design 360°.

The shop identity is an extension of Design 360°. A circle with the Chinese character ' 店 ' (shop) inside was placed next to the logo of the magazine, as a pair they reflect consistency under the same brand. The form of the circle originated from Chinese stamp marks and was used in different visual identity patterns across the applications.

HOME

FASHION

MUSIC

GOODS

EXHIBITION

BOOK

观念与设计店
CONCEPT
AND DESIGN
SHOP

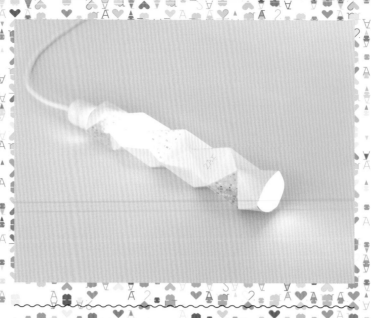

2Ar - Armunia Architects

DESIGN: JOSE CUNYAT

The naming and identity of Armunia Architects (2Ar) is meant to represent their sober, clean, elegant, elaborate, yet modern and dynamic architecture in which any sign of randomness is justified. One of the first goals was to strike a balance between those characteristics and the friendly, close, and personal attention they give their customers. To make the identity more valuable, Jose Cunyat developed dynamic logo-patterns that represent the principal goals and characteristics they were searching for.

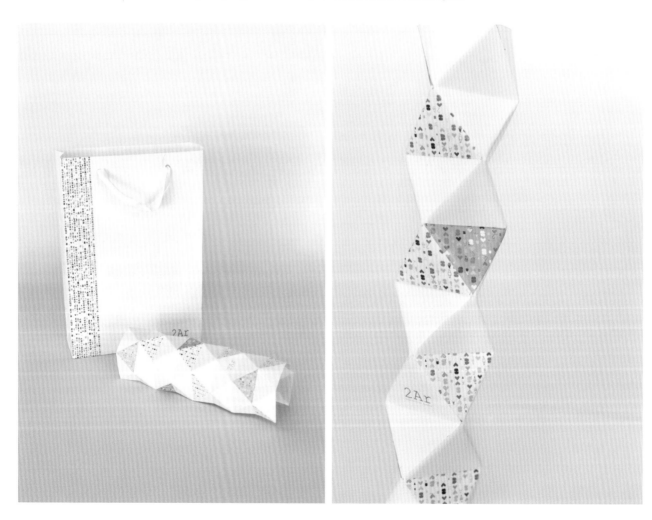

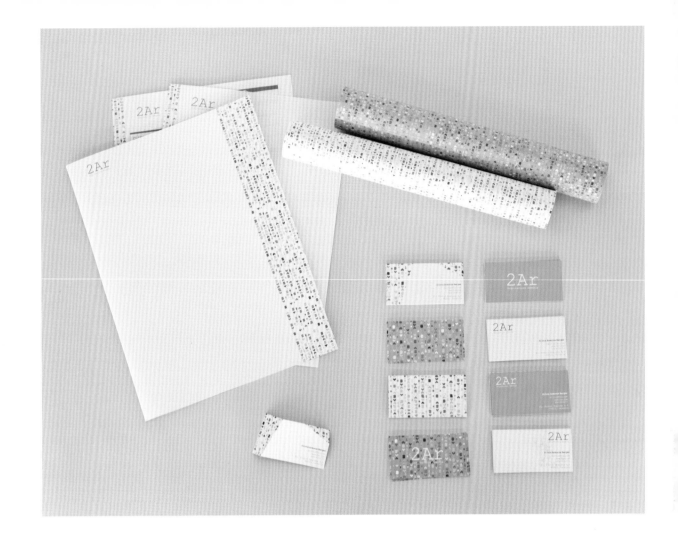

EMSE & ESME

ART DIRECTION: RAQUEL FIGUEIRA
DESIGN: RAQUEL FIGUEIRA

Raquel Figueira designed the identity and retail materials for the fashion designer including a logo and patterns for application in labels, stickers, gift boxes, and wrapping papers.

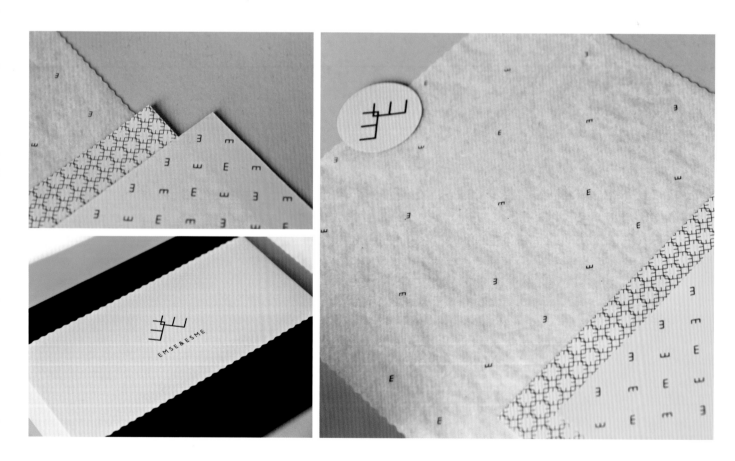

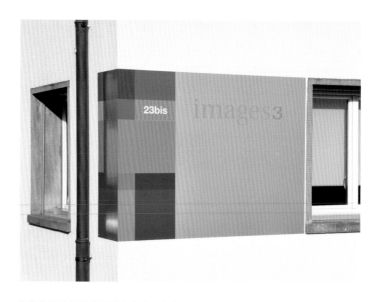

~~~~~~

Images3

~~~~~~

DESIGN: ENZED

The colored shapes illustrate the core activity of Images3, which
specializes in prepress and image retouching. Images3 works in the heart
of image making, where pixels become artwork.

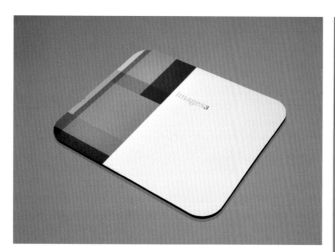

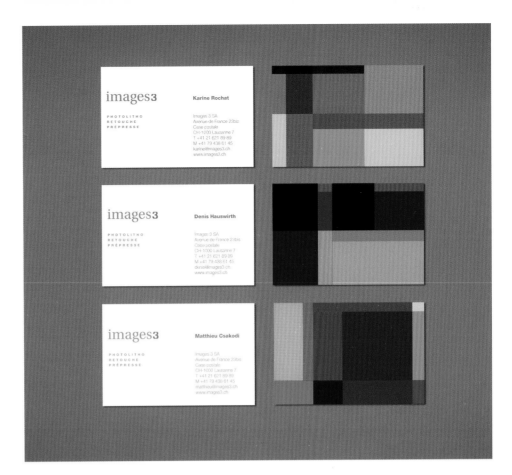

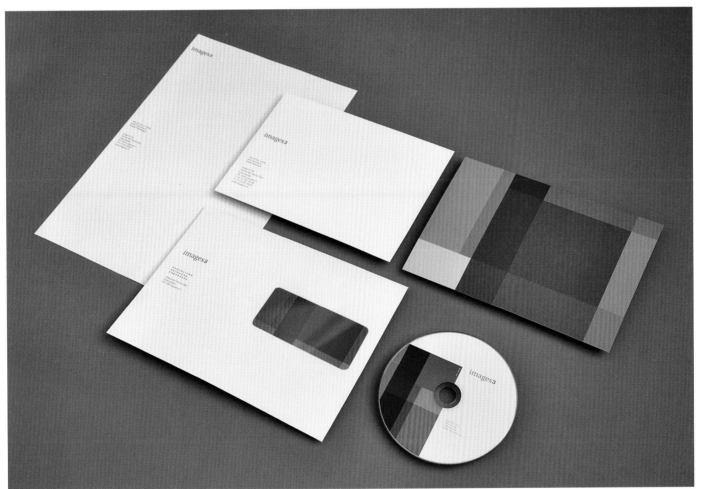

Young Guns of Wine Festival

DESIGN: 3 DEEP DESIGN

The Young Guns of Wine Festival gathers the best young winemakers from around Australia for a week long celebration of events throughout Melbourne's best and most interesting places to purchase and enjoy wine. The Young Guns of Wine initiative is about connecting and celebrating young wine makers and their exciting projects. Mavericks in their own right, they represent a bourgeoning and exciting section of Australia's premium wine industry. 3 Deep Design was engaged by Zebra Paradigm, the owner of the The Young Guns of Wine Festival, to establish a visual identity and creative positioning that provided a marked point of difference to all other events within the wine industry landscape. Capturing the energy, passion, and creativity of wine and winemaking, the positioning for the event presented the target market with a youthful and relaxed personality that was easily accessible and engaging.

Train of Thought

DESIGN: ABBY HAMBLETON

Abby Hambleton created the branding for Train of Thought, an art gallery that tours UK hospitals. The design uses colored lines based on those of a typical train map which are applied across a range of promotional materials including sketchbooks and pencils that are given to patients so they may create their own artwork.

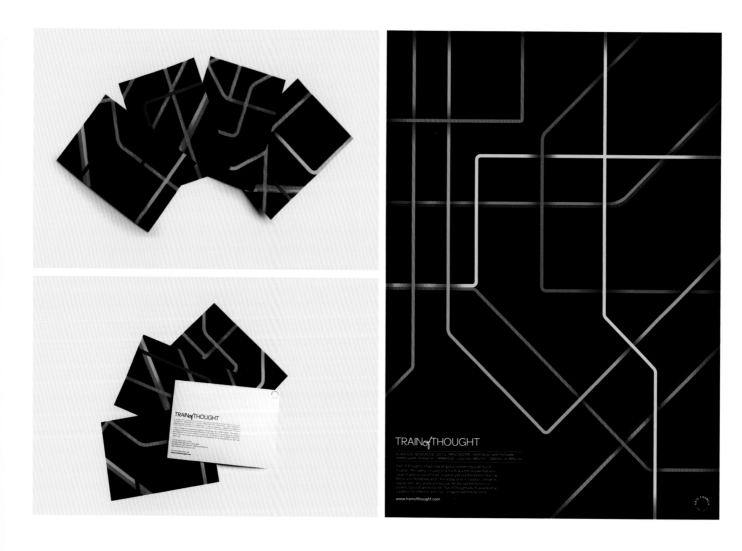

Bricos

DESIGN: ANAGRAMA

Bricos, originally known as Mayoreo Eléctrico Monterrey, had a very clear goal: to stop being a typical hardware shop and become a construction material supplier that could be perceived with much more formality alongside international competitors.

In order to develop the branding strategy, Anagrama thoroughly researched the project's commercial aspects and executed a deep brand diagnostic. This resulted in a solution that helps the company heighten their values such as service, honesty, responsibility, experience, and kindness, all of which have been key to the company's success throughout the years.

On the other hand, the company needed to attract qualified personnel, make these employees feel proud of working for Bricos, and give them a sense of belonging. The project's design decisions included creating a timeless brand with a completely different icon from any of its competitors They used a very clean typographic language and an institutional pattern that can easily be applied to any object.

These elements turn Bricos into a brand ready to compete internationally.

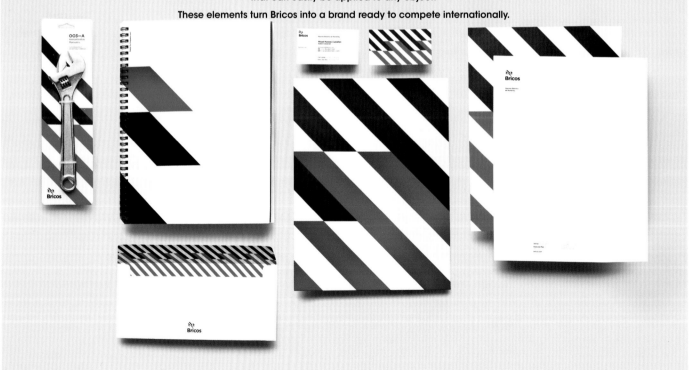

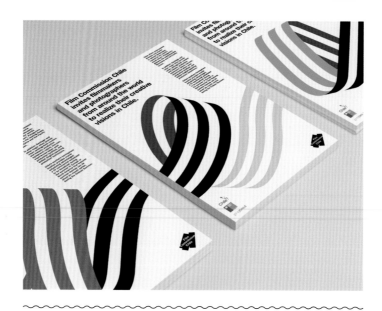

Film Commission Chile

DESIGN: HEY CREATIVE
DIRECTION: CRISTIAN JOFRE
PHOTOGRAPHY: ROC CANALS

The Film Commission Chile was created to promote Chile as a movie production destination, to help choose locations, to provide all kinds of services, and to be a link between the government and private companies. FCCh's visual identity was inspired by duct/gaffer tape. The tape is omnipresent in the world of movie production. Tape unites, joins, marks, holds, points, reminds, and aids work. Due to its flexibility, the lines and shape of the tape resemble the classic movie celluloid film. The image is drawn up in different directions, taking us to a dynamic universe that conceptually speaks to the FCCh linking mission. The variations in the color palette represent the diversity of landscapes found in the Chilean territory. The combined elements compose a unique image, with a well-defined personality, perfectly adapted to the conditions and objectives of the FCCh.

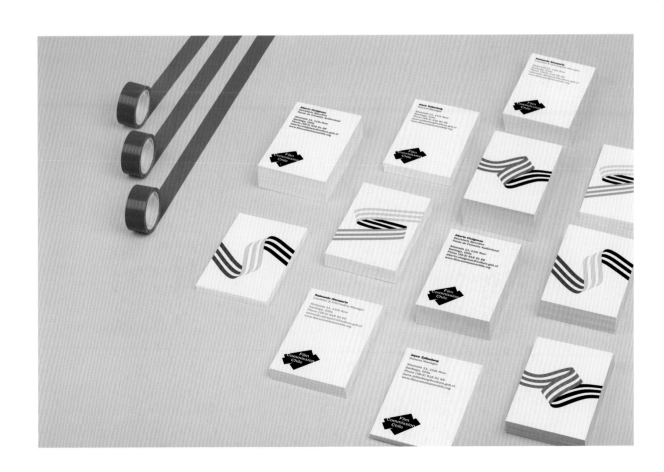

FIRMA + Kawaii

CREATIVE DIRECTION: ALEX MALYBAEV
DESIGN: KATERINA TETERKINA

FIRMA+Kawaii is a creative collaboration of FIRMA Design Agency's own series of products and Kawaii Factory's gifts and accessories. FIRMA+Kawaii launched a self-promotion project with a unique visual communication scheme.

Ravensbourne

DESIGN: JOHNSON BANKS
PHOTOGRAPHY: JAN MASNY AND MORLEY VON STERNBERG
BUILDING FAÇADE: FOREIGN OFFICE ARCHITECTS

johnson banks' approach was inspired by the building's façade - tessellating patterns of tiles after mathematician Roger Penrose. The fact that, from just three shapes, so many permutations were possible, seemed to nicely echo the education process. The team started experimenting with the institution's name thrown at angles through the tiles, originally neatly linking together. But they discovered that by slightly rotating the tiles, they could create a sense of movement and restlessness that seemed to fit well with the college's future ambitions. Incorporating the tiling pattern into student photographs gave the institution a unique approach to imagery too.

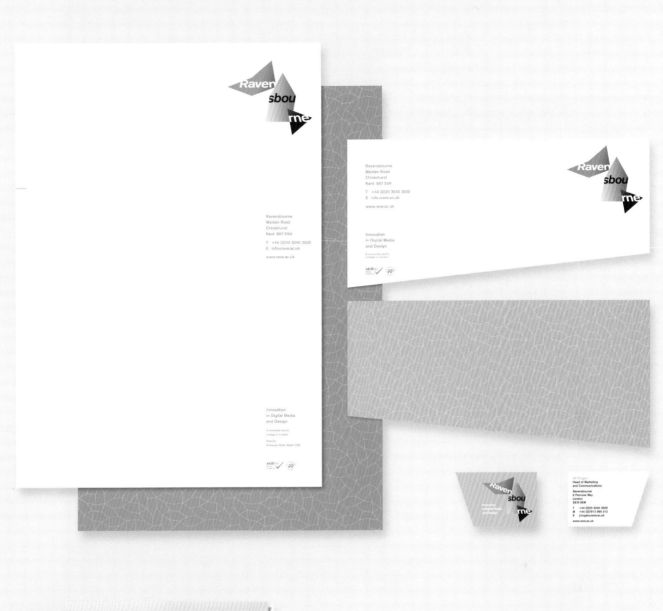

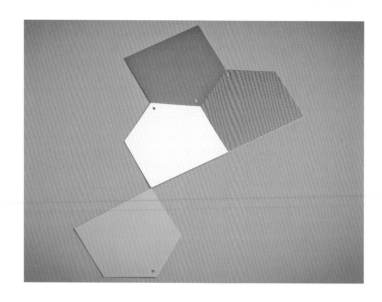

~~~~~~~~~~~~~~~~~~~~~~~~~~~~~~~~~~~

Dream

~~~~~~~~~~~~~~~~~~~~~~~~~~~~~~~~~~~

AGENCY: H55
DESIGN: HANSON HO

H55 designed the visual identity for Dream, a multi-label furniture design store.

To represent the idea of furniture and interior spaces, the universal house symbol was selected to represent the 'D' for 'Dream.' Inspired by Gerhard Richter's painting *4900 Colours*, they also created a landscape of houses in random colours for the identity's supporting graphics, to suggest Dream's distinctive open mindedness towards new up and coming brands and interior ideas.

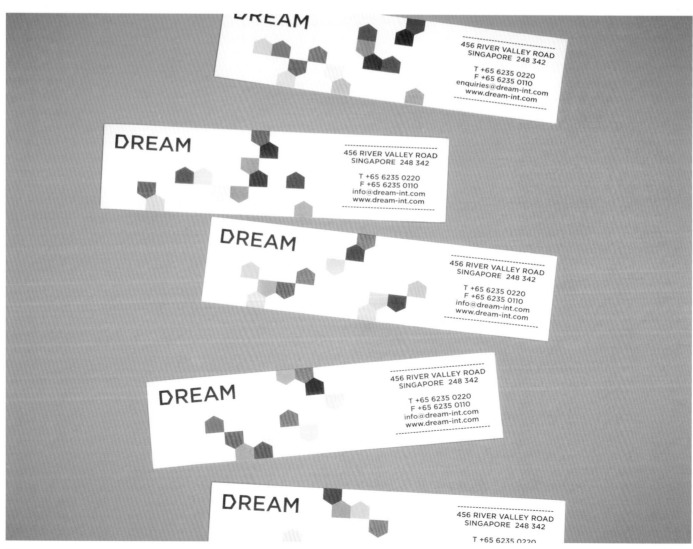

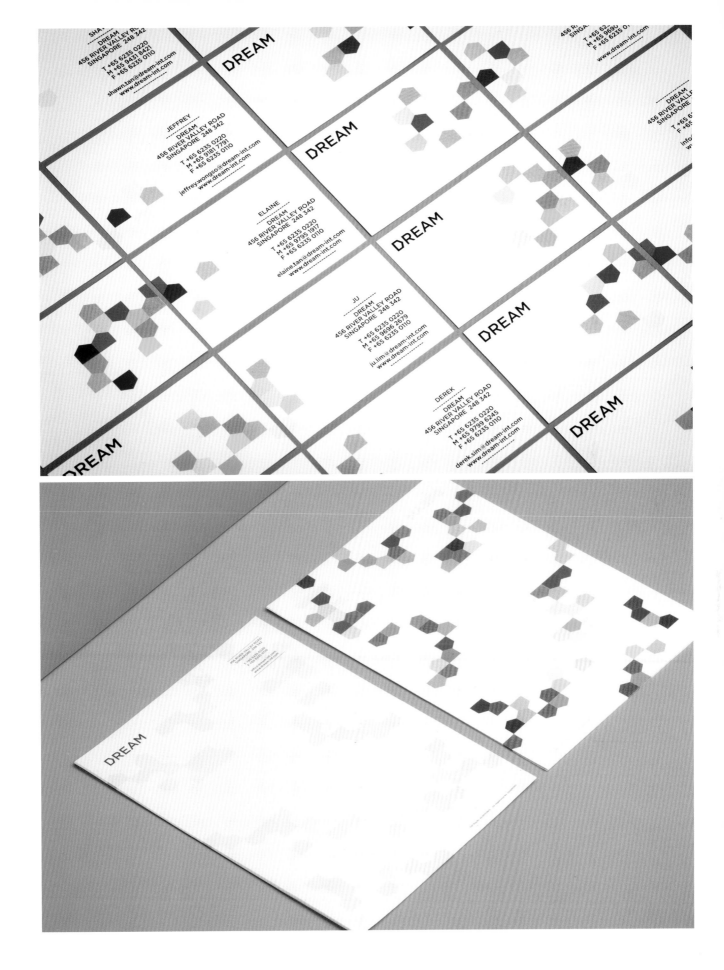

Devteq Software Solutions

DESIGN: DOMINIC LIU, KYOSUKE NISHIDA

Devteq Software Solutions is a software development company that serves organizations by providing web-based software solutions to streamline business processes. The logo is based on the shape of a QR code, and a pattern inspired by QR code elements was applied to various pieces of the branding material.

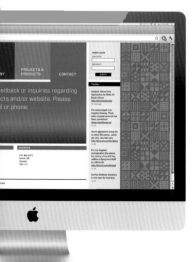

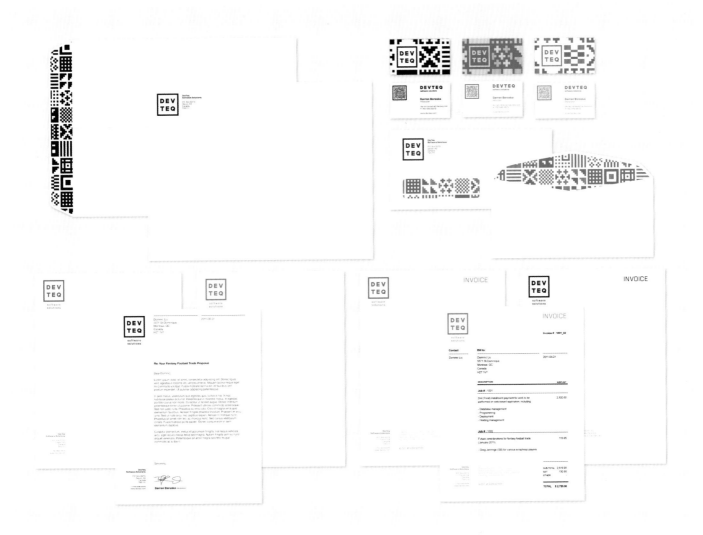

Nada

AGENCY: PLACE
CREATIVE DIRECTOR: ELOY KRIOKA

Nada, a production company, asked Place to develop a basic identity program. They designed the full pack of brand identity language elements and applied them to the whole system of brand supports. The identity consists of seven stationery pieces and the brand development guidelines.

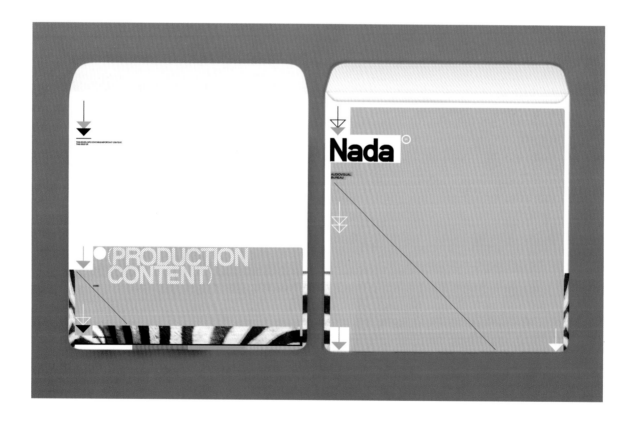

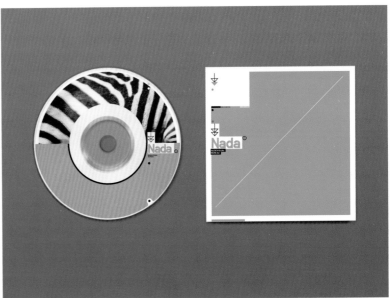

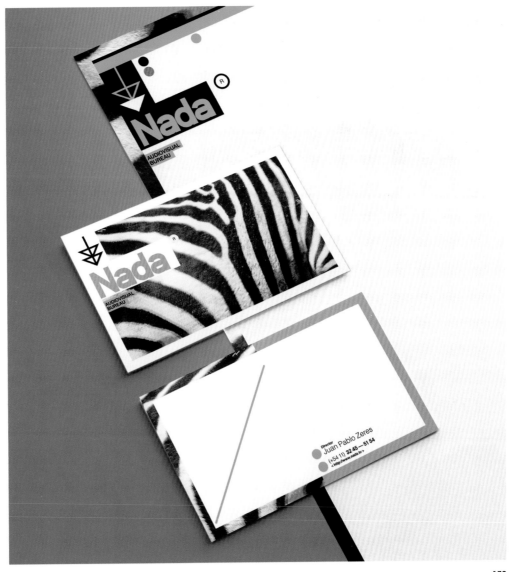

Unit Architects

DESIGN: JOHNSON BANKS

With its great name, johnson banks was convinced that Unit Architects could have something genuinely different within their market. Soon it became clear that the team could design a mark that directly reflected their name and their interest in modular design schemes by using a grid of six by six units. Right from the earliest presentations, johnson banks began exploring how the design could tile and tessellate into repeatable patterns. They also extrapolated the design principles out into headline typefaces and lettering.

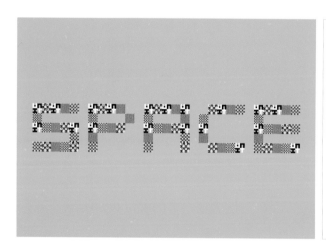

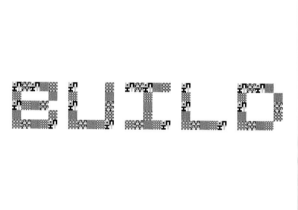

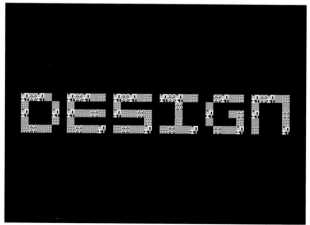

Unit Architects

Unit Architects

Unit Architects LLP
2nd Floor
36 – 37 Furnival Street
London
EC4A 1JQ

t 0207 199 7700
f 0207 657 4288

unitarchitects.co.uk

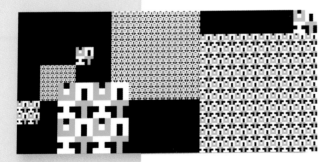

Unit Architects LLP
2nd Floor
36 – 37 Furnival Street
London
EC4A 1JQ

t 0207 199 7700
f 0207 657 4288
m +44 (0) 7810 893 306

unitarchitects.co.uk

Partner

Shangwei Image

AGENCY: LINSHAOBIN DESIGN
DESIGN: LIN SHAOBIN, MA XIAOQIN, CHEN XIAOQIANG

Shangwei Image is a photography studio that specializes in figure portraits and wedding photographs. Linshaobin Design designed a camera form from the letters of Shangwei as the core brand image.

K11 Design Store, Christmas 2011

AGENCY: BLOW
DESIGN DIRECTION: KEN LO
ART DIRECTION: KEN LO
DESIGN: KEN LO, CASPAR IP, CRYSTAL CHEUNG

BLOW was asked to design the main visual and promotional items for the K11 Design Store Christmas promotion. By combining different modern forms, they created a contemporary, colorful, and festive Christmas tree.

Micheline Branding

AGENCY: ANAGRAMA

Micheline is a print-shop boutique dedicated to designing and printing stationery and pieces for social events. Interested in rejuvenating the brand in order to reach a new audience of young adults, Micheline came to Anagrama.

Identity and Packaging for Saks Fifth Avenue

AGENCY: PENTAGRAM
DESIGN: MICHAEL BIERUT

Saks Fifth Avenue, the quintessential cosmopolitan retailer, approached Pentagram seeking an all-embracing solution for its visual brand. The challenges were many: the solution needed to be traditional yet contemporary, appeal to men as well as women, and somehow project an "unmistakably Saks" image.

The solution was to revisit one of the calligraphic logos that the store had used for much of the last 50 years. Divided up into details, the newly redrawn logo immediately becomes bold and modern. Every part contains a reminder of the whole, creating a visual language that can be used to unify everything from shopping bags to storefronts and interiors.

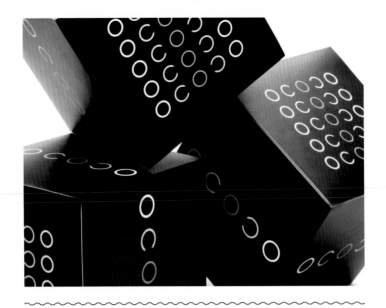

~~~~~~~~~~~~~~~~~~~~~~~~~~~~~~~

OCOCO

~~~~~~~~~~~~~~~~~~~~~~~~~~~~~~~

AGENCY: FIREFLY BRANDING
CREATIVE DIRECTION: JIWON SHIN
PHOTOGRAPHY: JAROSLAV KVITZ

To become the next break-through fashion brand in Korea's mass online market, OCOCO needed a dynamic visual identity. Accordingly, a creative approach that communicates a contemporary brand identity was developed. Using the tagline "Updated Basic," an amazingly simple design concept imbues classic items of clothing with a contemporary flair. The brand name is presented in an eye-catching, black-and-white typographic design. It is symmetrical yet gradient, sophisticated yet playful, and classic yet contemporary.

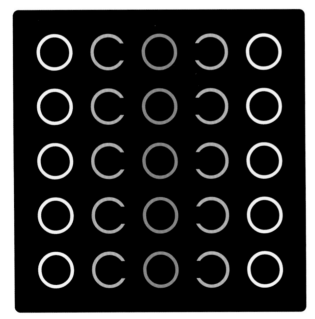

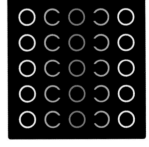

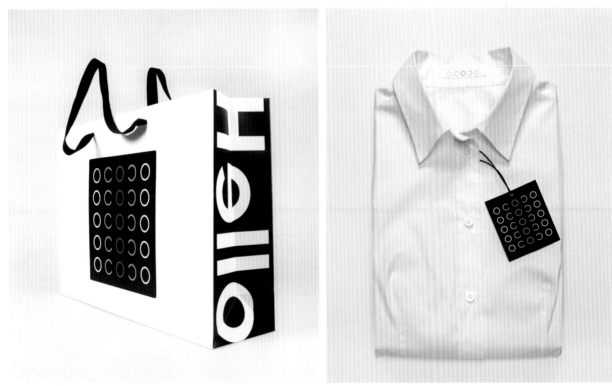

Saks Fifth Avenue "Think About..." Campaign

AGENCY: PENTAGRAM
ART DIRECTION: MICHAEL BIERUT
DESIGN: MICHAEL BIERUT, JENNIFER KINON, JESSE REED

For the 2010 spring campaign Saks Fifth Avenue introduced a new tagline, "Think about...," a playful suggestion that shoppers consider new ways to play with their personal style via various items found at Saks. The tagline was finished with amusing statements about fashion and style: "Think about... belting a new tunic with your husband's old tie" and "Think about... making your creative side your outside." If the tone seems a little familiar, it should: the campaign was inspired by the maxims published by legendary fashion editor Diana Vreeland in her "Why Don't You..." column for Harper's Bazaar magazine.

The designers created a witty visual corollary for the campaign. The "Think About..." logo complemented the black and white squares of the Saks Fifth Avenue identity, as well as the right angles and modularity of the identity's grid-based design. Each of the ten letters in "Think About..." was given its own block in the logo. These in turn corresponded to ten individual printed catalogs, each in the shape of its block. The letters on the catalog covers were reversed for fun, creating simple black and white illustrations of collected items, like shoes (the "B," for "Think about...Banning Boring" catalog), watches and jewelry ("K," for "Think about...Karats"), and buttons ("O," for "Think about...Occasionally Outdressing Others.").

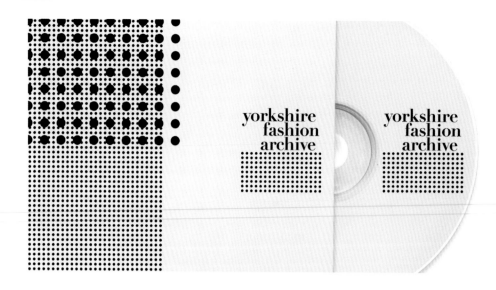

Yorkshire Fashion Archive

AGENCY: TREBLESEVEN
CREATIVE DIRECTION: DAVID WATSON

Based in the School of Design and underpinned by research excellence in textiles at the University of Leeds, the Yorkshire Fashion Archive is a new, publically accessible collection of haute couture, fashion garments, and everyday clothing. It provides a unique historical and cultural record of Yorkshire life and documents clothing produced, purchased, and worn by Yorkshire folk throughout the 20th Century.

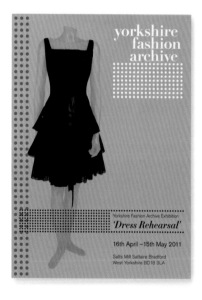

KARL LAGERFELD FOR
CHANEL HAUTE COUT

yorkshire
fashion
archive

50's
Style

Yorkshire
Fifties Fashion

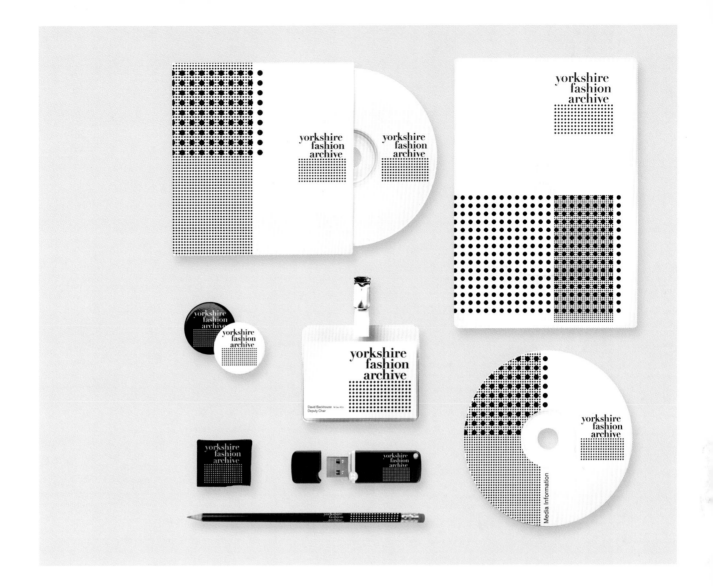

Belmacz

DESIGN: MIND DESIGN

Belmacz has opened its first shop and gallery in London Mayfair. For this reason the original identity was re-designed and Belmacz worked in collaboration with Jump Studios on the interior.

The new identity takes the original logo but adds a variety of thicker, 'raw' letter shapes. Those shapes relate to the process in which raw minerals and diamonds are refined until they become a piece of jewelry. The visual references start with the mines, go to the raw materials, the raw letter shapes, and in the end to the refined letter shapes of the original logo.

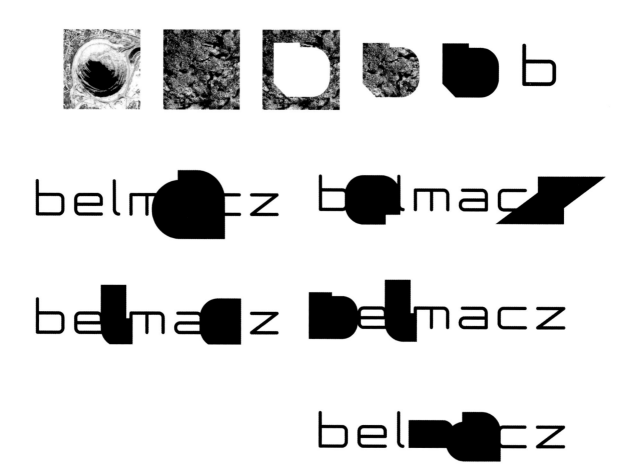

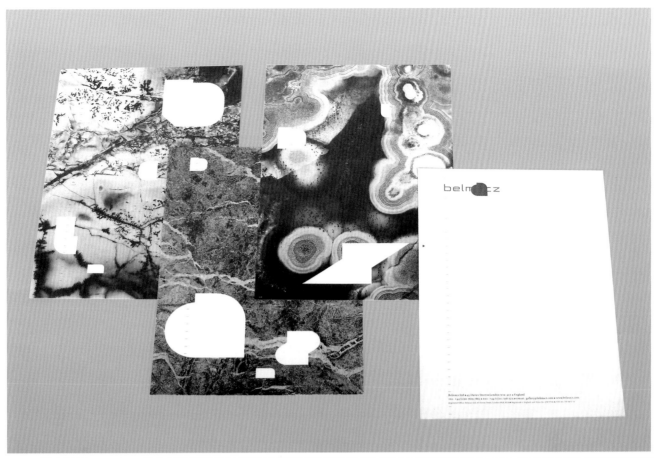

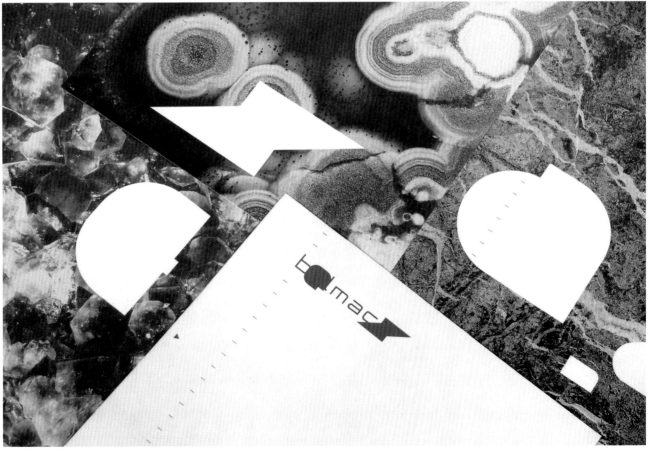

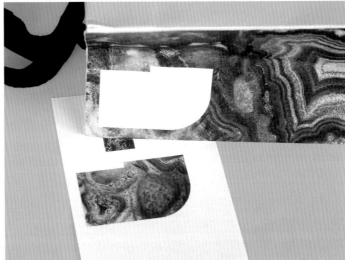

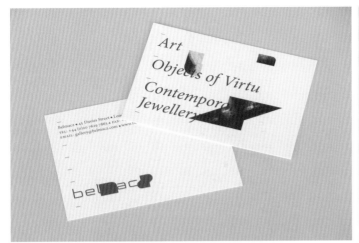

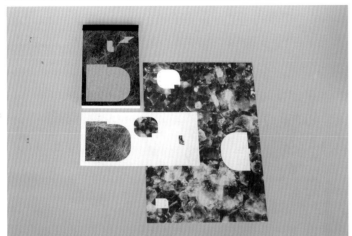

~~~~~~~~~~~~~~~~~~~~~~~~~~

Circus Idenity

~~~~~~~~~~~~~~~~~~~~~~~~~~

DESIGN: MIND DESIGN

Mind Design designed the identity for Circus Identity, a new club and restaurant with a burlesque theme and changing performances. Since the club's interior features many mirrored surfaces, the design of the logo is based on the shape of a kaleidoscope. The outline shape and basic construction of the logo always remains the same while the inside changes depending on its application. Other influences came from Surrealism, Art Deco, Alice in Wonderland, animals, and the steps leading up to the large table that doubles as a stage. A main feature of the interior is a 3-dimensional version of the logo built from different layers of perspex, set into a wall and illuminated from the back in changing colours. This project was a collaboration with Design Research Studio.

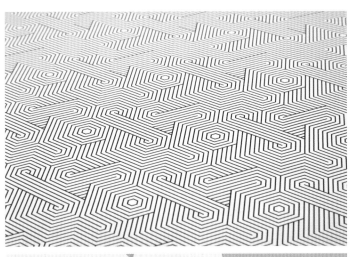

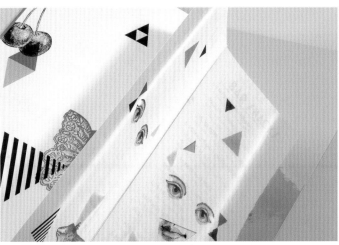

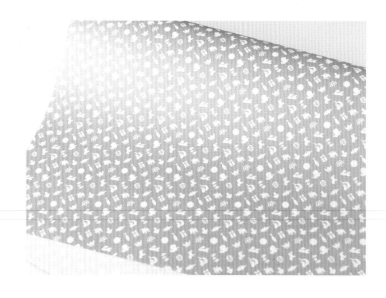

~~~~~~~~~~~~~~~~~~~~~~~~~~~~~~~~~~~~~~

Piccolina

~~~~~~~~~~~~~~~~~~~~~~~~~~~~~~~~~~~~~~

ART DIRECTOR: RYO UEDA (COMMUNE)
DESIGN: RYO UEDA (COMMUNE), MANAMI INOUE (COMMUNE), DAISUKE TAKADA, YUJI
TERADA
COPYWRITER: KOSUKE IKEHATA
PRINTING DIRECTOR: MANAMI SATO

Piccolina is a Scandinavian antique shop that offers a variety of collectibles. One of the reasons antiques are so appealing is that they preserve an aspect of the values or culture from people living in a different period. Each antique item tells customers something about Scandinavian history or culture. 14 different Scandinavian icons are used to form the shop logo, which may be used on a range of promotional tools, such as wrapping paper, direct mailings, and Sapporo shop signage. Each of the icons represents an important piece of history and it can all be found at Piccolina.

Recycled

DESIGN: GOSIA CZYSZCZON

Recycled is a brand created for a studio that designs and produces all kinds of housewares such as textiles, wallpapers, prints, and stationery. All the products are characterized by unique patterns inspired by fauna and flora. Ecology and natural life are the defining ideas of Recycled. The funny patterns they apply to everyday objects evoke joy, warmth, and positive energy in addition to providing interesting variety.

Souvenirs for KPSS

ILLUSTRATION AND DESIGN: KATARINA MRVAR, LUKA MANCINI (LUKATARINA)

The identity was based on illustrations inspired by the existing logo, salt production, and the natural habitat preservation aspects of the park. The illustration can be multiplied in horizontal and vertical directions. The first phase was to compose a visual bank of all the relevant flora and fauna and salt production elements which are also used independently or as a pattern on some applications. The identity found its place on a number of promotional products and packaging like badges, magnets, notebooks, tea cups, boxes, paper bags, umbrella, T-shirts, etc.

Möoi

AGENCY: SEVENTHDESIGN™
DESIGN: BRUNO SIRIANI

Möoi is part of a new concept in Buenos Aires: contemporaneous food. This wave has been merged in this project with modern art & design to build a nice space that is comfortable and impressively utilizes a large number of different shapes, textures, and colors. SeventhDesign™ developed a huge number of graphic pieces such as business cards, various letterheads, stickers, packaging, food and wine menus, etc., and many industrial pieces for the interior and the exterior of the space.

The brand elements, graphic design, packaging, and industrial design provide a strong image to this beautiful restaurant located in Belgrano, Buenos Aires.

~~~~~~~~~~~~~~~~~~~~~~~~

Kofetika Coffee Shop

~~~~~~~~~~~~~~~~~~~~~~~~

DESIGN: DÉNO LELIĆ

Déno Lelić designed the corporate identity for Kofetika, a boutique coffee shop.

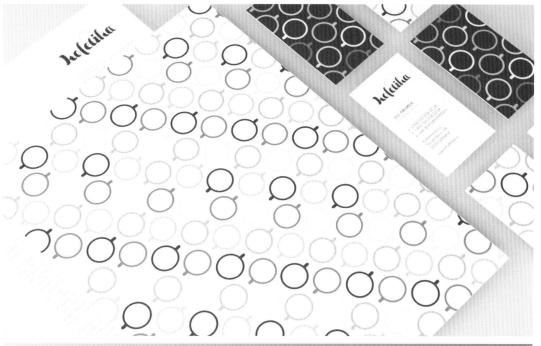

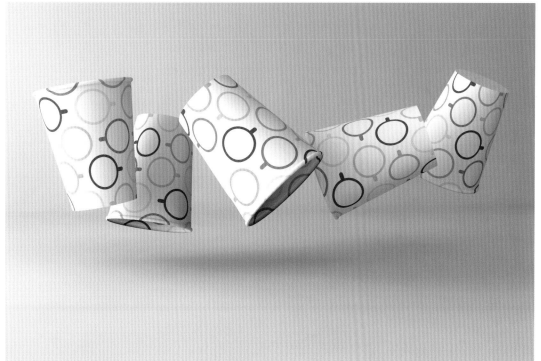

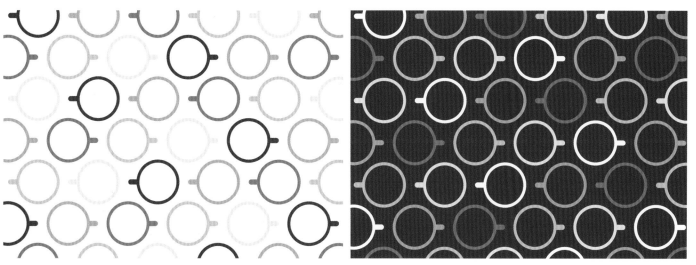

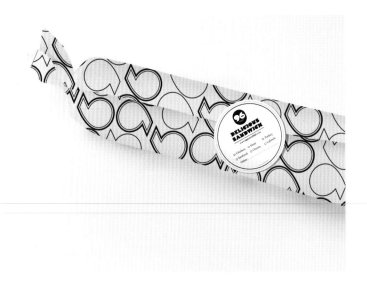

~~~~~~

Uptown966

~~~~~~

DESIGN: LEA HESHME

Uptown966 is a Mediterranean fusion upscale café in the KSA. The name was inspired by the location of the restaurant and its area code.

The identity is based on black foil printed rough brown cardboard to reflect the genuine, sophisticated yet down to earth image the restaurant wanted to convey, along with seamless patterns based on the word "uptown" and the number "966." The simplicity outlines the "savoir-faire" of the group behind that concept, and makes it accessible to business people as well as families.

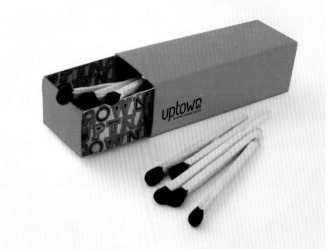

Brill.

AGENCY: COUPLE
DESIGN: ZANN WAN, KELVIN LOK

Brill is a food take-out business using small shop spaces in dense urban settings where consumers want to be amused and dazzled while expecting care and attention. The branding melds precision with frivolity to surprise and delight. The logo starts with a scalloped border and moves inward with Greek fret motifs to checkers and cross-stitch. The subtle repetition of the pattern carries a sense of temperance, like juggling for the queen.

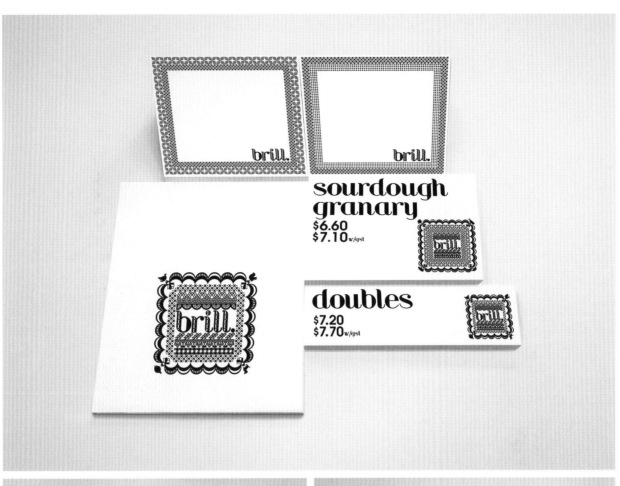

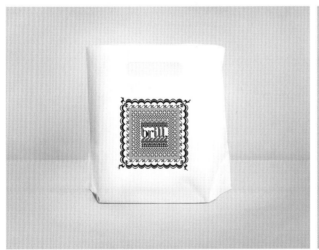

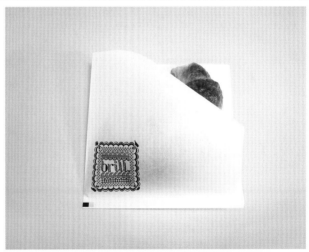

POP Noodle

DESIGN: CREATIVE INC

POP Noodle is a pop-up Asian street food restaurant and takeaway located in Dublin, Ireland. The objective of POP was to create a brand identity, which could be implemented quickly and cost effectively, whatever the location. Sitting on an angle in a red circle with perforated edges, the logo mark has the capacity to be applied to anything quickly and cheaply.

The patterns used throughout the interiors and on the brand's printed materials were inspired by Pop art and especially the work of Roy Lichtenstein. The simple groupings of different sized circles work together to create a simple yet effective design feature.

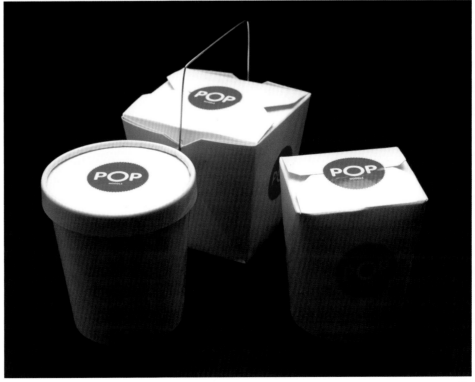

Vasconcelos 980-1 Sur
San Pedro Garza García
64000 México

+52 (81) 8342 3979
+52 (81) 8999 3253
+52 (81) 8243 4240

www.fundidora.com

FUNDIDORA.

Vasconcelos 980-1 Sur
San Pedro Garza García
64000 México

+52 (81) 8342 3979
+52 (81) 8999 3253
+52 (81) 8243 4240

www.fundidora.com

Fundidora

DESIGN: ROD CASTRO

Rod Castro designed the branding for Fundidora, a sophisticated artisan chocolate boutique.

FUNDIDORA®

FUNDIDORA®

Vasconcelos 980-1 Sur
San Pedro Garza García
64000 México

+52 (81) 8342 3979
+52 (81) 8999 3253
+52 (81) 8243 4740

www.fundidora.com

Vasconcelos 980-1 Sur
San Pedro Garza García
64000 México

+52 (81) 8342 3979
+52 (81) 8999 3253
+52 (81) 8243 4740

www.fundidora.com

FUNDIDORA®

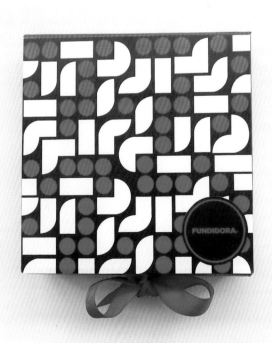

Box Café

AGENCY: ALT GROUP
CREATIVE DIRECTION: DEAN POOLE
DESIGN: TOBY CURNOW, JANSON CHAU
WRITER: DEAN POOLE, BEN CORBAN

Box Café is located at the entry of New Zealand's largest performing arts centre. It functions as an information centre, a ticketing office, and a venue. The name and visual identity needed to communicate the offering simply. The name says what it does.

The logomark was built from of a series of dots that reference the design vernacular of theatre lighting and dot matrix printers, commonly found in ticket offices.

The mark lends itself to a range of executions and finishes: printed, diecut, embossed, recessed, or floated. This was extended into a broader visual language communicating the offering pictorially.

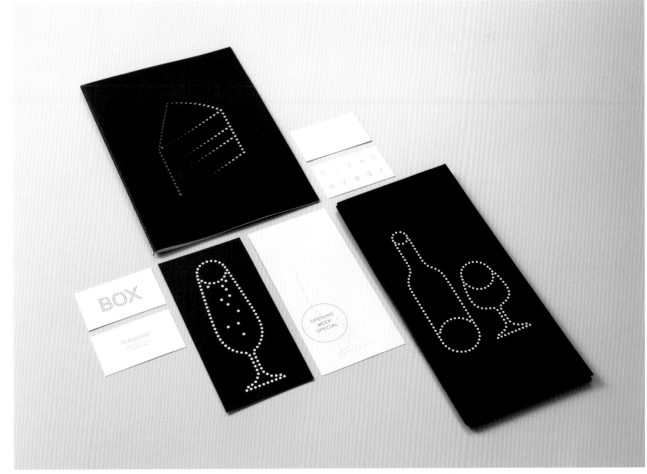

TOMORROW

~~~~~~

Tomorrow

~~~~~~

AGENCY: BIG HORROR
ART DIRECTION: ALEXANDROS MAVROGIANNIS
COPY: MARILENA GEORGANTZI

Tomorrow is a newly established bag brand dedicated to making your connection to nature easier. Feel free to walk, run, and dive in mountains, valleys, and lakes because Tomorrow is designing exactly what you need.

The Odrzańska Bryza Football Team

DESIGN: PIOTR HOŁUB

Piotr Hołub designed a comprehensive visual identity for the football team of the Fine Arts Academy Odrzańska Bryza.

The first challenge was to create a simple mark that would be both distinct and noticeable. Next, the remaining promotional materials such as business cards, letterheads, and fan merchandise were developed and described in detail in a brand manual. Additionally, a series of eleven promotional illustrations was created to depict the team's general character.

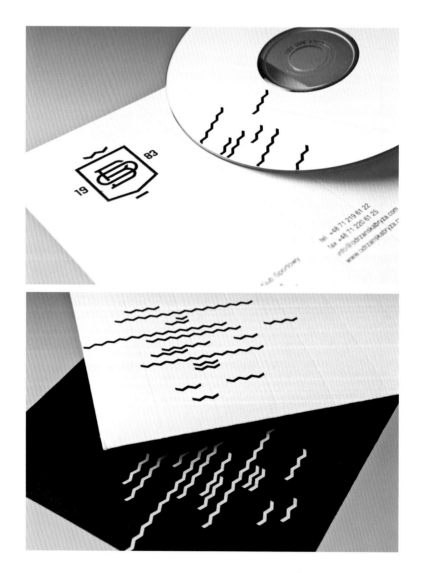

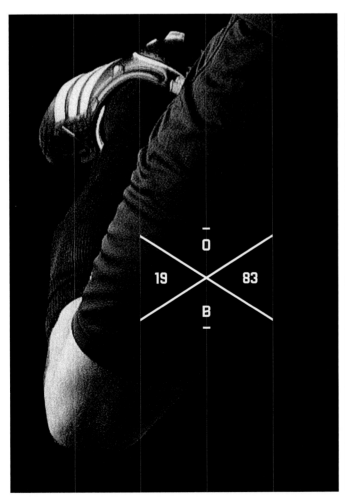

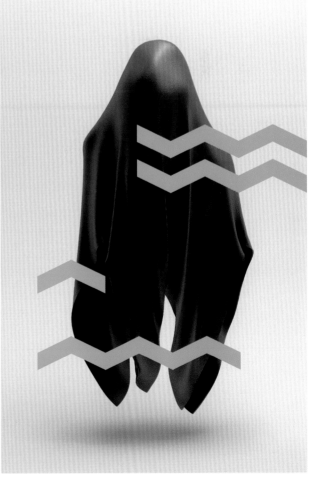

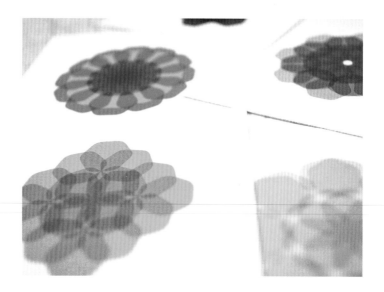

~~~~~~

IXORA

~~~~~~

DESIGN: SHUBHAM SHREYA

Ixora is a cosmetics brand largely based on the concepts of ayurveda. Ayurveda is a system of traditional medicine in India. The design concept tries to position Ixora as a brand that is modern yet rooted in history. The logo represents a combination of the 5 elements of the physics ayurveda subscribes to - air, water, fire, earth, and ether. The brand language takes the harmonious balance between these elements forward with the help of forms that are elegant and simple. Forms are created with permutations and combinations of basic elements from the logo, based on a regular pattern. Much like the boundless scope of ayurveda, it puts forth the possibility of creating infinite patterns.

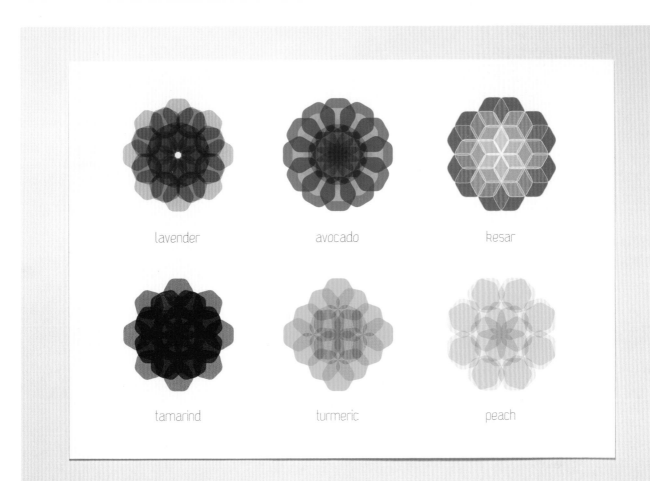

lavender · avocado · kesar

tamarind · turmeric · peach

BODY MIST
with lavender base

100 ml

ixora

ixora

MOISTURISING FACE CREAM
with peach essence

100 gms

~~~~~~

Union

~~~~~~

DESIGN: RED DESIGN

Union approached **Red Design** to create the brand identity for a contemporary costume and bridal jewelry store.

The challenge was to create something that felt both classic and contemporary.

With a very broad set of uses proposed for the identity, from hallmark to packaging and signage, the team felt it important to create a multifaceted identity with elements that could be used together or individually. The identity is made up of 4 main elements: 1. a logotype, 2. an accompanying symbol 3. a graphic derived from the symbol, and 4. an extensive bold colour pallet, offset by muted accent colours.

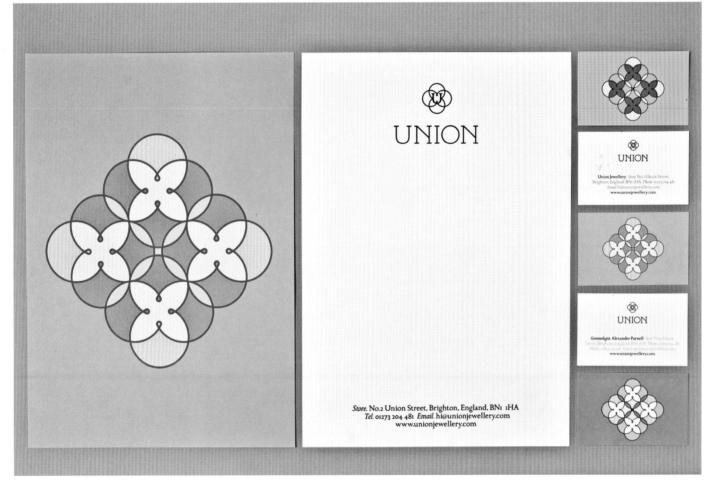

INDEX

Codefrisko

www.codefrisko.be

Codefrisko is a graphic design & art direction studio founded by Audrey Schayes (founder of Frisko design) and Thomas Wyngaard (co-founder of Code Magazine Belgium) in 2006. Codefrisko's clients work in culture, fashion, architecture, design, and the food industry. Their expertise ranges from acting as a think tank to doing graphic design, photos shoots, providing online solutions, and much more.

In order to achieve these goals, they sometimes collaborate with experienced professionals, web developers, interior architects, or photographers, depending on the needs of a project.

Commune

www.commune-inc.jp

Commune, a creative team based in Sapporo, Japan, has been mainly active in graphic design. The theme of creation for them is to make something better. Inspired by the will to make something better, their design work may move people or it may make society work a little better. It's like giving a gift. They choose a gift with the idea of delighting that special someone. It's a pleasure for them to be able to present something the recipient doesn't expect and truly appreciates. At times, Commune's creations take people by surprise, awaken their emotions, or even move them to tears. That's exactly what they're looking to create.

Couple

www.couple.com.sg

Founded in 2007 by two designers, Couple encompasses a broad scope of design activities, including designing for the written word and moving image, designing exhibitions, the ordering and identity of urban spaces, and designing for corporate communications and branding.

Creative Inc

www.creativeinc.ie

Formed in 1996, Creative Inc is a Dublin based multi-disciplinary creative agency, specializing in brand identity, design, and advertising. Their approach to their work is simple and honest: they place an emphasis on creativity and conceptual thinking, turning their passion for what they do into commercial success for their clients, large and small. They approach their work with enthusiasm, optimism, and conviction. Every project is seen as an opportunity to push boundaries and create distinctive and engaging work. They are driven by a sense of responsibility, both to their clients and the environments where their work is ultimately seen and enjoyed.

Daisy Dayoung Lee

dayounglee.com

Daisy Dayoung Lee, a New York based graphic designer, was born and raised in Korea. She studied Visual Arts and Design at Seoul National University and got a master's degree in communications design at Pratt Institute in New York, USA.

DED Associates

www.dedass.com

DED is a nose to tail creative agency with a hard-earned reputation for being innovative, adaptable, influential, and extremely effective.

Established in 1991, DED is a start-up that has been around for years, continually exploring the new, whilst asserting an uncompromising attention to detail.

Demian Conrad Design

www.demianconrad.com

Created in 2007, the Demian Conrad Design studio is based in Lausanne, Switzerland. Working mainly in the cultural field and the leisure industry, the studio lends its expertise to everything related to events, communication, and visual identity. As a multi-disciplinary entity, the studio favours a "lateral thinking" approach with the aim of finding creative, destabilizing solutions and forms of avant-garde, cutting-edge, hard-hitting communication. Projects successfully carried out by the studio include the identity of the Gabbani brand, the campaign for the Lausanne Underground Film Festival, the innovative approach of the Blackswan foundation as well as projects for conferences such as TED and the Forum des 100.

Déno Lelić

www.denolelic.si

Déno Lelić is a young graphic designer from Ljubljana, Slovenia. He mainly works with printed matter, from creating strong visual identities to packaging and editorial design.

Design Ranch

www.design-ranch.com

Design Ranch is a nationally recognized design agency, specializing in lifestyle branding and corporate collateral. The team doesn't pitch hay, they pitch ideas. They are fully committed to a comprehensive creative process from start to finish and everything in between. Whether they are delivering thoughtfully integrated solutions for existing brands or developing unique solutions for start-ups, they know how to make companies giddyap.

Dominic Liu & Kyosuke Nishida

dominicliu.com
kyosukenishida.com

Dominic Liu is a Montreal-based graphic designer. Kyosuke Nishida is a Toronto-based graphic designer.

They frequently collaborate on a wide range of multi-disciplinary design projects, from branding and identity work to tactile installations.

Edgar Bąk

www.edgarbak.info

Edgar Bąk works for various ad agencies. He primarily designs magazines. He worked as an art director of FUTU DESIGN GUIDE and PURE magazine, for which he won the Chimera and KTR.

He is also a graphic designer at WAW magazine, a quarterly Kultura Popularna and the film industry magazine FILMPRO. He graduated with honors from the Warsaw Academy of Fine Arts, Faculty of Graphic Arts (diploma in professor Lech Majewski's studio, 2006) where he was an assistant professor in the illustration studio of Professor Zygmunt Januszewski.

Edge Design

www.steve-edge.com

At Edge Design they believe in relationships: with Edge Design's clients, and with their brands. And brands, like people, need to build special relationships with the people they are talking and selling to.

The most important thing for any brand is to be remembered. If people think of you when they're deciding what to buy, there's a chance they'll spend their money on your product or service. Edge Design's approach involves tapping into your company's DNA, finding the treasure that nobody else has and using it to create branding that sticks in people's minds.

ENZED

www.enzed.ch

ENZED is a design consultancy founded in 2001 by Nicolas Zentner in Lausanne, Switzerland. It specializes in editorial, corporate, and cultural design.

Facetofacedesign

facetofacedesign.be

Since 2008, Flore and Delphine have joined forces to form Facetofacedesign, a multidisciplinary graphic design studio based in Brussels, Belgium.

They appreciate that each project comes with its own set of singularities, demanding a different, project-specific approach each time. They will take on projects of all sizes. They analyze demands and find solutions through their various experiences.

p.014-015

Firefly Branding

www.fireflybranding.com

Jiwon Shin, an internationally acclaimed brand designer, is the Founder and CEO/Chief Creative of Firefly Branding. Firefly is headquartered in New York City and also has offices in Prague and Seoul, opening Firefly in Paris in 2012. She has directed over 80 major branding programs in a diverse range of industries and is the recipient of numerous international design awards. Jiwon also created and launched the exhibition, "Connecting New York – Prague – Seoul," an initiative designed to connect different cultures through the medium of design.

p.190-191

gardens&co.

www.gardens-co.com

gardens&co. is a small independent graphic house. The team members mainly come from 3 areas: graphics, visual merchandising, and web design. Every project undertaken is crafted with passion. They build partnerships with the clients to understand their communication challenges. Applying their design thinking to develop thought-provoking solutions to address commercial needs, they provide a one stop service from enhancing corporate brand image to customers' shopping experience.

p.130-131

Gosia Czyszczon

www.gosiaczyszczon.com

Gosia Czyszczon is a graphic designer and illustrator living and working in Cracow, Poland. After finishing her studies in graphic design in 2010, she started to cooperate with many agencies as a freelance artist and joined the Rebeliarts team. While studying, she improved her traditional drawing and painting skills which have been very helpful in creating digital art. Mostly inspired by nature, vintage children's illustrations, and custom lettering, she creates colorful, simple, and joyful illustrations.

p.206-207

Grant-ru Li

grant-li.com

Lava Beijing is led by Grant-ru Li. After graduating from CAFA, he was invited to work in the Fabrica-Benetton Communication Research Center, Italy for one year. After Fabrica, he went to Amsterdam and worked at Lava Design in 2011. Now he is Creative Director of Lava's Beijing branch.

p.028-029 , p.086-087

H55

www.h55studio.com

Hanson Ho is an award winning Creative Director who works under the studio name of H55, which he founded in 1999. Since then, Hanson has created numerous visual identities, brand applications, and publications which have represented Singapore on an international level.

Featured by the Sunday Times as one of the top Graphic Designers in Singapore, Hanson has received recognition and awards from some of the most prestigious international design competitions for his works, including the British D&AD, New York Type Directors Club, New York One Show Design, Creative Circle Awards, Tokyo Type Directors Club, and the New York Art Directors Club.

p.090-091, p.092-093, p.174-175

HelloMe

www.tillwiedeck.com

HelloMe is a Berlin based design studio focusing on art direction, graphic design & typography.

With a systematic design approach the studio creates and implements innovative communication strategies and distinctive dynamic visual systems for cultural, social, and business clients. The studio's mentality is ideas led, project specific, and grounded in analytic thinking.

HelloMe believes that design is experimental, dynamic, and useful. Therefore, they approach each commission individually from a cross media perspective, and emphasize the intrinsic characteristics of each project to create innovative, well-crafted design solutions and self initiated projects with a passion for detail and typography.

p.095

Hey Creative

heystudio.es

Hey is a multidisciplinary design studio based in Barcelona, Spain specializing in brand management and editorial design, packaging, and interactive design.

The team shares the profound conviction that good design means combining content, functionality, graphical expression, and strategy. As a result, they offer their clients a personal service based on mutual understanding and trust, working to innovate from rationality and directing advice to meet actual needs.

p.168-169

Hype Type Studio

www.hypetype.co.uk

Formed in 1999 by Paul Hutchison, Hype Type is a multi-disciplinary graphic design and communications studio with over 10 years experience working closely with local, national, and international clients.

With offices in both the UK and the US, Hype Type Studio has built a reputation for producing relevant, memorable, and effective creative solutions.

p.115

Hyperakt

www.hyperakt.com

Hyperakt is an independent NYC design firm with a passion for creating work that effects change in the world around us: meaningful design for the common good. Hyperakt works with clients who fight for justice, celebrate culture and diversity, spread knowledge, and engage in social entrepreneurship. Their most recent work includes projects for the Ford Foundation, Girl Scouts, UNICEF, GOOD magazine, and ClimateWorks. As Harvard Business Review says, "by having a bigger purpose it just might be that Hyperakt's building a 21st century design studio: the crucible of big, world-changing ideas." Hyperakt's founding principals Deroy Peraza and Julia Vakser lead a tight-knit team with varied expertise and a passion for design. The studio is based in Brooklyn.

p.060-061

Jiyoung Lee

www.iamjyl.com

Jiyoung Lee is a graphic designer who studied art and design in New York City. After his graduation from Pratt Institute (Communication Design) he worked/freelanced for various design agencies. Now he is back in his home country, Korea, working for one of the biggest portal webs called Daum Communications. In his designs, he always tries to achieve a conceptual as well as aesthetic point of view.

p.108-109

johnson banks

www.johnsonbanks.co.uk

johnson banks is a London-based design consultancy with a global reputation. Set up in 1992 by Michael Johnson, the company works on design projects as varied as airline rebrands (Virgin Atlantic) and world famous museums (The Science Museum in London), art centres in Philadelphia and Paris, and a space observatory in Japan. Their experimental typography in Japanese and Chinese has been exhibited in Shanghai and their recent 3D typography, Arkitypo quickly became a worldwide internet phenomenon.

The company has consistently shown that a small group of designers and thinkers can consistently solve the thorniest business problems with world-class solutions, whilst demonstrating wit, intelligence, and humanity along the way.

p.172-173, p.180-181

Jose Cunyat

www.josecunyat.com

Jose Cunyat is an interdisciplinary graphic and product designer based in Berlin. With a passion for what he does, he delivers relevant, considered, and engaged work.

p.156-157

Joshua Gajownik

www.joshuagajownik.com

Joshua Gajownik believes design is the intersection of art, humanism, and science; the result of observation and experimentation through three lenses; a combining of the emotional and the empirical.

p.070-071

Katerina Teterkina

www.behance.net/re_it_it

Katerina Teterkina is a graphic designer from Moscow, Russia. She specializes in identity, logos, and packaging. Now Katerina works as an art director in ARCTICA design studio.

p.170-171

Kateryna Mishyna

www.behance.net/katerynamishyna

Kateryna Mishyna is a 23-year-old junior designer. Born in Russia, the Portuguese designer currently resides in Lisbon. She obtained her bachelor's degree from Fine Arts University of Lisbon. Kateryna is currently finishing her master's in communication design and is searching for an internship or job in or outside Europe. Graphic design is her passion, the way she express her ideas and herself through the artistic statement.

p.020-021

Kayla Jang

www.kaylajang.com

Kayla Jang is a graphic designer based in NYC, focusing on printed matter, identity, environmental graphics, along with explorations in digital media.

p.144-147

Kelvin Qu

www.roncham.com

Kelvin Qu is a member of New York Art Directors Club, ICOGRADA, CDA, CCII Collective, Founder and Creative Director of Roncham Design Office.

Kelvin's works focus on brand management of the retail, FMCG, and corporate branding, etc. Many have been accepted to show in various international design competitions.

p.050-051

KentLyons

kentlyons.com

We are a design agency
We are visual communicators
We are digital specialists
We are brand consultants
We are an advertising agency
We are KentLyons

KentLyons creates communications that are beautiful and useful without compromise.

They've created some interesting projects for some well-known companies such as Channel 4, the BBC, Macmillan, the D&AD, Sky, the Design Museum, LV=, Swiss Re, Film London, ITV, Westfield, Foster + Partners, and many others.

p.026-027

Kilómetro Estudio

www.kilometroestudio.com.ar

Kilómetro is a young visual communication studio, specializing in branding and visual identities. With experience in branding, packaging, editorial, web design, motion graphics, and visual design, it is not characterized by a style, but by the constant search for excellence in what they do.

Kilómetro also develops its own brand of clothing, KM, which allows you to experiment and exploit their strategic and creative ability, special collections, such as VISUAL BY KM, where they cross all areas that make up a visual identity.

p.024-025

La Lonja Gráfica

www.lalonjagrafica.com

La Lonja Gráfica is a graphic design studio founded by Cristina Carrascal and Joaquín Gómez in 2011. They provide a full range of branding and design services. They combine smart thinking and wide-eyed strategic creativity in a highly collaborative fashion, producing great ideas and fresh solutions that bring great results to all types of businesses.

They think design should be a subtle, simple, and honest concept, which lasts over time because it has the size and the message appropriate for its content.

La Lonja Gráfica's work covers: graphic design, editorial design, visual identity, web design, signage, and so on. They take art direction, design, development and project management from beginning to end.

p.036-037, p.074-075

Lava

www.lava.nl

Lava is an Amsterdam based design agency, founded in 1990. They have strong roots in editorial design, which has trained them to work as visual storytellers. Over the years, this way of thinking has led to a unique approach to identity and communication design.

Lava's creative team consists of graphic, motion, and interactive designers that work for a diverse range of clients from the commercial, governmental, non-profit, and cultural sector.

p.052-055, p.082-083

Lea Heshme

www.behance.net/heshmelea

Lea Heshme is a Lebanese graphic designer currently working at WonderEight, a boutique-style studio located in Beirut, Lebanon. Living in the world's most multi-cultural city, Lea has constantly found endless inspiration in the people around her. Her city is filled with "joie de vivre," diversity, history, love, pain, and promises, which makes it easy for her as a designer. WonderEight is one of the leading branding agencies in Lebanon and takes branding to the next level; with over 25 successful concepts in Lebanon and abroad. Here they do branding, corporate identities, advertising campaigns, packaging, furniture, illustrations, animations, and even restaurant interior.

p.214-215

Li Qi

blog.163.com/seven_mr

Li Qi graduated from Art Faculty in Huashang College of Guangdong University of Business Studies in 2010. After graduation, she was employed by a design studio. In 2011 she participated in Wuhan Intuition Poster Exhibition and her work has been permanently collected by Wuhan Art Museum. Her works have won many prizes in the design field.

p.084-085

Linshaobin Design

www.linshaobin.com

Lin Shaobin is a Shantou based creative from Guangdong, China. He is a top 10 designer of Guangdong. With eight years' experience, he is the chief designer and art director of Linshaobin Design Studio.

p.182-183

Lo Siento

www.losiento.net

Lo Siento is a small studio that especially enjoys taking over the whole concept of the identity projects.

Its main feature is an organic and physical approach to the solutions, resulting in a field where graphic and industrial design dialogue, always searching an alliance with the artistic processes.

p.066-067

Lukatarina Design Studio

www.lukatarina.net

Katarina Mrvar and Luka Mancini (Lukatarina Design Studio) deal with various problems in the area of visual communications. With knowledge and talent, they try to contribute to the improvement of society and the environment, thus creating for clients who are aware of the environmental, social and corporate responsibility. In parallel, they develop their own self-initiated educational and research projects. They have received numerous awards (Brumen award for Luka's thesis, Brumen recognition for Katarina's type Simtype, Brumen award for a series of posters Marine renegades of the Slovenian coast, Prešeren Award for Luka's Master thesis Philloguerrilo). Their work can be seen in many international design books (Tres Logos Los Logos, Logo Lounge 1, 3 and 4, Graphic Design Inspirations) and magazines (IdN).

p.208-209

Maria Pershina

www.behance.net/Mary_P

Maria Pershina graduated from the British Higher School of Art and Design "Visual Communications" in 2011. Now she is Art Director of Design Bureau 360 gr in Moscow, Russia.

p.034-035

Marnich

www.marnich.com

Marnich is a design and communication consultancy based in Barcelona. They believe in simplicity and clarity. Their clients range from small restaurants, independent publishers, and music festival to large corporations, banks and museums.

p.100-101

Martin Albrecht

international-man-of-danger.com

Martin Albrecht graduated from The Graphic Arts Institute of Denmark in 2009 after several years as a design professional.
Today, working as Creative Director in Copenhagen, he focuses on creating a strong visual language for his clients, which are both recognizable and inspirational.

p.040-041

Márton Hegedűs & Kristóf Kőmíves

www.behance.net/martzihegedus
www.behance.net/komiveskristof

Márton Hegedűs and Kristóf Kőmíves are two designers from Budapest with complementary ideas. They both study graphic design at the Hungarian University of Fine Arts.

p.080-081

Maythorpe

www.maythorpe.com

Maythorpe is a creative studio based in Melbourne Australia. It's a unique team of designers, art directors, and all-round creative thinkers specialising in identity, print, and web.

p.012-013

Mayúscula

www.rociomartinavarro.es

Mayúscula is a design studio in Barcelona founded by Rocío Martinavarro, specialized in the creation of brands of any complexity and format.
Mayúscula in Spanish is an upper case character, a majuscule used to start a sentence or to remark a concept. It stands out, and that's their main goal for their clients and brands: to exceed the average, using creativity as a strategic tool.
In the past two years, their design has helped start-ups like PanPan, Wemories, and Kuwaity Zeri Crafts, as well as established companies such as PepsiCo, Neinver, or the Dutch MN Services and Rabobank. Rocío Martinavarro has over ten years of experience working in New York, Amsterdam, and Barcelona, for companies like Summa Brand Consultancy (National Design Prize), Patrick Thomas, or Edenspiekermann, designing visual identities such as the Spanish Broadcast Corporation (RTVE), la Caixa Savings Bank, Barcelona TV, Adif o Mútua Terrasa, among others.

p.110-111, p.112-113

Milkxhake

www.milkxhake.org

Milkxhake is an independent graphic design studio located in Hong Kong since 2006. Founded by Chinese graphic designer Javin Mo, Milkxhake advocates the power of visual communication from visual branding, identity, print, and website by bringing up creative ideas and visual languages. Not solely applying graphic design, the team focuses on the creative process while delivering messages to their collaborators as well as public community.

p.152-155

Mind Design

www.minddesign.co.uk

Mind Design is a London-based independent graphic design studio founded by Holger Jacobs in 1999 after graduating from the Royal College of Art. The studio specialises in the development of visual identities and has worked for a wide range of clients in different sectors.

p.150-151, p.198-201, p.202-203

Mucho

www.mucho.ws

Mucho is a visual communications and graphics studio.
Its work consists in disciplines such as art direction, strategic and corporate identity, editorial design, packaging, graphic communications, digital design, and motion graphics.
Mucho values the visual ambition of projects as much as the commercial will, and considers excellence its permanent objective. Ideas are at each project's heart and all work is done with the intention of it being unique, with a constant effort to avoid repetitive formulas.
Mucho's singularity and diversion, and the sum of different partners offer a rich variety of solutions and a wide space for critical shared thoughts. The closeness between the partners and their clients is indispensable and the know-how of the clients is basic for the construction of the projects.

p.138-141

Neue Design Studio

www.neue.no

Since its establishment in 2008, Neue Design Studio has created visual communication with the belief that insight and creativity are equally important in the process of creating engaging, long-lived concepts. Working from their 6th-floor studio with its overview of Oslo, they develop strategies, make editorial design, brand identities, packaging, and illustration for both print and screen.

p.042-043

OXNU Design

www.oxnu-design.com

OXNU design studio is a creative agency based in Brisbane, Australia and also Shenzhen, China.
The team works across the various fields of graphic design, advertising, photography, website, and video. They work internationally to help companies develop their brands. Their experience spans creative ideas and solves design problems in real business.

p.118-119

Pentagram

www.pentagram.com

Pentagram is the world's largest independent design consultancy. The firm was founded in 1972 and is run by 16 partners, a group of friends who are all leaders in their individual creative fields. Working from offices in London, New York, Austin, and Berlin, the firm specializes in different areas of graphic design, industrial design, and architecture, producing printed materials, environments, products, and interactive media for a wide range of international clients.

p.120-121, p.188-189, p.192-193

Piotr Hołub

peha.com.pl

Piotr Hołub is a graduate of the faculty of design at the Academy of Fine Arts in Wroclaw, Poland. Currently he is working as a graphic designer at Mamastudio, a brand design studio based in Warsaw. Prior to Mamastudio he gained experience in such agencies as Kolman Advertising and Media Ambassador. He's been awarded and recognized many times on design industry sites such as bahance.net and cpluv.com, as well as the prestigious "Best of Nation" award for his erasm. us logo in the Wolda competition, 2011.

Place

www.weareplace.com

Place is a creative studio that works with ideas applied to design experiences. Place means projects for any kind of support.

During the last years Place worked for important consultants, where they developed projects concerning all branches related to designing. The team got to meet great artists and designers, and together, they went through different fields, from advertising to animation, from graphic campaigns to environment design. Such experience got them to create their own environment, a space wherein they can mix both art and creativity, concepts and design: Place.

Raquel Figueira

www.raquelfigueira.com

Raquel Figueira is a Portuguese designer who lives and works in London, UK.

Since graduating from the MA Communication Design at Central Saint Martins in 2010, she's been working as a freelance designer and illustrator mainly for fashion and retail clients alongside her self-initiated projects.

She also produces photography and set design work and publishes a visual inspiration blog.

Red Design

www.red-design.co.uk

Established in 1996 and based in Brighton, UK, Red made its name by producing award winning graphic design for the music industry.

They now work across a range of diverse sectors delivering high quality still, moving, and interactive design.

Their integrity and passion for beautiful and effective design is reflected in the work they do. They love and believe in what they do.

Rejane Dal Bello

rejanedalbello.com

Senior Graphic Designer & Illustrator Rejane Dal Bello has been based in The Netherlands since 2004. Originally from Rio de Janeiro, she began her career working for renowned branding & design companies in Brazil.

After her BA in Graphic Design in Rio de Janeiro, Rejane went on to study under Milton Glaser at the School of Visual Arts in New York City. She completed a MA at Post St Joost Academy in The Netherlands in 2006. During her MA, Rejane joined Studio Dumbar, a graphic design studio that has established a unique position in the Dutch Design scene.

Rejane is currently a Senior Design at Studio Dumbar, as well as a member of the faculty of Post St Joost Academy, where she teaches Graphic Design and Creative Process.

Relè Agency

www.agenziarele.it
www.sonnoli.com
www.tassinarivetta.it

Relè Agency is located in Rimini, on the east coast of Italy. It works with Studio Tassinari/Vetta and its Art Director Leonardo Sonnoli.

Rod Castro

www.rod-castro.com

Rod Castro, creative designer and director, graduated from Universidad de Monterrey and Art Center College of Design, specialized in brand development and creative solutions.

Romualdo Faura

romualdofaura.com

Romualdo Faura currently works as a freelance graphic designer in Murcia, Spain, doing projects for his clients as well as for other design studios in Spain, France, and the USA.

He focuses on corporate branding, icon design, illustration, and editorial projects.

He also has been teaching graphic design at various universities and design school in Mexico, Guatemala, and Spain.

Ruiyi Design Office

www.ruiyids.com

Ruiyi Design Office is an advertising and design studio in Changsha, Hunan Province, China.

Samantha Kim

www.samantha-kim.com

With her wide-ranging interests in everything from package design and branding to photography and surface design, Samantha Kim uses her love for the arts to bring creativity to all her experiences in New York City. Prior to her career in the city, Samantha studied at the Rhode Island School of Design where she earned a BFA in Graphic Design. She is also a native of the Seattle area and takes her upbringing in the beautiful northwest as inspiration in her simple yet eye-catching designs.

SEA Design

www.seadesign.co.uk

SEA is an award winning brand communications agency working across all media.

Their reputation for innovative and effective design touches all disciplines from brand strategy and positioning, corporate identity, brand art direction, and digital media.

Their understanding of how brands are created has amassed international clients such as Adidas, Selfridges, Jamie Oliver, EMI, Matthew Williamson, King Sturge, Global Cool, and Maitland.

SeventhDesign™

www.seventhdesign.com.ar

SeventhDesign™ is a graphic designer studio based in Buenos Aires, Argentina, creating customized and ambitious solutions for national and international clients for almost 7 years.

With expertise in identity, print, packaging, interactivity, and environments, the SeventhDesign™ studio crafts initiatives that integrate multiple disciplines.

Through wide-ranging capabilities and extensive reach, they coordinate programs that address the spectrum of a client's needs from a unified perspective. This work helps facilitate communication between client stakeholders, resulting in adaptable systems that define visual communication across an organization.

Shubham Shreya

www.behance.net/shubhamshreya

Born in the year of the snake during summer, Shubham Shreya loves the spring season and dogs. She graduated from the National Institute of Design, Ahmedabad (India) as a graphic designer and like most other designers, she loves to illustrate, click photographs, and travelling.

Singular

wearesingular.mx

"WE ARE SINGULAR.
DIVERSITY IS OUR MAIN STRENGTH.
WE ARE THINKERS, ANALYZERS, SOLVERS, AND REVOLUTIONARIES."

A creative studio from Monterrey Mexico, Singular strives in pushing the envelope. Never constrained by the mainstream, their team is always on the lookout for unique ways to engage an audience.

Curious about the way things work, they are constantly renovating. Graphic design, architecture, photography, animation, fashion, music & world affairs are all sources of inspiration. They understand the way each element connects with the public and have the sensibility to create memorable experiences that ultimately evolve into tangible results.

p.018-019

Studio Egregius

studio-egregius.com

Studio Egregius is a multidisciplinary design studio, doodling while kerning, painting while writing, snapshooting while die-cutting, coding while rendering, googling while daydreaming, self-caffeinating while brainstorming, working hard while keeping sane. Studio Egregius was founded in 2009, by Le Huy Anh and Nguyen Quang Trung. They are concept-based and creativity-led.

They listen, listen, research, research, research, brainstorm, research, create, listen, refine, listen more, refine some more, until the work is done. They are hungry for success and won't settle for less.

p.124-125

studio fnt

www.leejaemin.net

Jaemin Lee has been working as an art director at studio fnt which he found in 2006. Lee is a lecturer at Seoul National University, Seoul Women's University, and Kaywon School of Art & Design, and had special lectures at the University of Seoul, Seoul Women's University, Hongik University, and Seoul National University. He also gave a lecture at CA conference and Sangsangmadang forum in Seoul. Lee participated in many exhibitions including "TYPOJANCHI 2011: International Typography Biennale," "Design Korea 2010," "Connected Project" in Graphic design festival Breda, "Weired Book," etc. Lee was the winner of 2010 Reddot Design Award and Web Award Korea. His works and interviews were featured in many media publications, such as "Typography Workshop 6," Design magazine," "g: magazine," "CA magazine," and so on.

p.058-059

SVIDesign

www.svidesign.com

SVIDesign (London) was established by Sasha Vidakovic as an independent studio after 20 years of working as a creative director with the world's most respected branding consultancies in London and Milan. An international list of clients from luxury, lifestyle, fashion, interiors and architecture, food and drink, automotive, and healthcare, partner with SVI Design on branding, packaging, graphic design, and digital media projects. SVIDesign demystifies the process of branding by taking a rigorously analytical but straightforward approach to research, sector analysis, and unique customer insight. This helps to develop observations about a brand's challenges based on clear facts and market evidence. Then once the science stops, the magic begins. The list of clients amongst others: Victoria Beckham, Taschen, Harrods, Azimut-Benetti yachts, THORN, Lakeland, WWF amongst others.

p.114, p.116-117

Toormix

www.toormix.com

Toormix is a Barcelona-based design studio specialising in branding, art direction, creativity, and graphic design, set up in 2000 by Ferran Mitjans and Oriol Armengou. They carry out corporate identity, editorial, print, web, and communication projects for a wide variety of clients, from small graphic pieces to global branding and communication projects.

Their way of working is based around strategic collaboration with the client. Starting from information and ideas, they develop a clear and coherent creative discourse in order to reach people through innovative and visually attractive design proposals.

At Toormix they play with brands, because playing means not being afraid, always going that bit further, taking on new challenges, questioning approaches, and blazing new paths.

p.122-123

Trebleseven

www.trebleseven.com

Trebleseven is an independent design studio based in South West London. The team works closely and openly with their clients - gaining a thorough understanding of each project's unique needs before creating appropriate and distinctive designs that communicate and engage with the intended audience. They are mainly engaged in graphic design and art direction, brand identity and development, print design and communications, design for digital media, etc.

p.194-197

VBN

www.vbn.hk

VBN is a vivid and innovative design company. Its professional fields unite graphic design, environment consideration, products development, multimedia, and other areas of work under one platform. VBN always provides well-rounded solutions for the brand designing, with its main focus on innovation and experience.

p.106-107

WE ARE ALL IN THIS TOGETHER™

www.waaitt.dk

WE ARE ALL IN THIS TOGETHER™ is a multidisciplinary design studio located in the city centre of Copenhagen. The studio was established by graphic designers Anders Rimhoff, Jess Jensen & Dennis Müller in the summer of 2011.

The name indicates their approach to working with clients and projects. They value a close and personal relationship with their clients because they believe that this creates the best results.

WAAITT™ works with visual identities, typography, design for print (posters, books, magazines, stationery, brochures, etc.), websites, photography, video, art direction, and creative consulting.

p.032-033

Graphic design studio by Yurko Gutsulyak

gstudio.com.ua

Yurko Gutsulyak is a design professional with 10 years work experience. In 2005 with his sister Zoryana he founded Graphic design studio by Yurko Gutsulyak. Studio was awarded more than 50 awards, such as European Design Awards, Red Dot, Epica Awards, Golden Drum, Communications Arts, HOW, and many others. Yurko Gutsulyak is actively involved in the development of the local design and advertising market. He is President of the Art Director Club Ukraine; moreover he represented Ukraine in the jury of different international advertising and design festivals. In 2010 he was invited to be lector at European Design Conference (Rotterdam, Netherlands).

p.098-099, p.128-129

ACKNOWLEDGEMENTS

We would like to express our gratitude to all the designers and companies for their generous contribution of images, ideas, and concepts. We are also very grateful to many other people whose names do not appear in the credits but who made specific contributions and provided support. Without you all, the successful completion of this book would not have been possible. Thank you for sharing your innovation and creativity with all our readers around the world.